MARKETING MANAGEMENT

DR. M. VAANMALAR | J. SRI KEERTHANA

Contents

Syllabus

Unit-I

Introduction- definition- concepts – Markets – Types – Marketing Management – Marketing Manager, Duties and Responsibilities.

Unit – II

Function of Exchange – Buying and Selling - Functions of Physical supply – Facilitating functions – Marketing Finance – Marketing risk – Marketing Information – Transport – Storage – Warehouse – Grading – Standardisation – Buyer Behaviour – Buying motives

Unit – III

Selection of distribution channel – Wholesaler – Function of Wholesalers – Retailers – Functions- Elimination of Middleman.

Unit – IV

Differences between product Marketing and Service Marketing – Pricing of Services – Problem of Services Marketing.

Unit – V

Sales Promotion – Introduction – Need – Method- Advertisement Meaning and definitions – Objectives – Kinds – Product and Non- Product Advertisement – Manufactures own Advertisement and Advertisement Agencies - Tele Marketing – E-Marketing

I

Introduction to Marketing

Introduction

Marketing manages distinguishing and meeting human and social necessities. Probably the briefest meaning of marketing is —meeting needs profitably‖. The target of all business undertakings is to fulfill the requirements and needs of the general public. Promoting is, in this way, an essential capacity of all business firms. At the point when a salesman sells clothes washers, a specialist treats a patient or an Administration requests that individuals take their kids for getting polio drops, each is advertising something to the objectives.

Generally, little firm proprietors didn't give as much significance to marketing as to different capacities, for example, bookkeeping, creation and selling. Preparing programs, endeavor advancement and the current push for intensity have now given high need to advancing marketing mindfulness among entrepreneurs, and promoting is presently expecting its legitimate spot alongside other business capacities.

Since mid 1990s there has been an adjustment in the considering financial specialist from item direction to buyer direction. Current business concerns lay accentuation on _selling satisfaction' and not just on selling items. The exercises must be composed to build up the advertising blend, which gives greatest fulfillment to the clients.

That is the reason marketing examination and item arranging possess a significant part in advertising. The other significant elements of marketing include: purchasing and collecting, selling, normalization, pressing, putting away, transportation, advancement, estimating and hazard bearing. Hence, the extent of promoting is wide and not any more confined to simply selling of items.

Meaning and Definition of Marketing

The term "Marketing "is derived from "Market", which can be defined as – "a place where buyers and sellers gather to buy and sell the products". But Marketing is not only about selling; because in order to sell the product we must know the needs (basic requirements) of the customers.

The concept of marketing can be viewed from social and managerial perspectives. So Marketing is a social and managerial process by which individuals and groups obtain what they need and want through creating and exchanging products and value with others. At its simplest, marketing can be defined as exchange transactions that take place between the buyer and the seller. Marketing is the management function, which organizes and directs all those business activities involved in assessing and converting customer purchasing power into effective demand.

We shall be learning later in the lesson that marketing is more than a mere physical process of distributing goods and services. It is the process of discovering and translating consumer wants into products and services. It begins with the customer (by finding their needs) and ends with the customer (by satisfying their needs). The components of marketing concept are as under:

1. **Satisfaction of Customers:** *In the modern era, the customer is the focus of the organization. The organization should aim at producing those goods and services, which will lead to satisfaction of customers.*
2. **Integrated marketing:** *The functions of production, finance and marketing should be integrated to satisfy the needs and expectations of customers.*
3. **Profitable sales volume:** *Marketing is successful only when it is capable of maximizing profitable sales and achieves long-run customer satisfaction.*

So, —Marketing is the performance of business activities that directs the flow of goods and services from producer to consumer or user.‖ This definition is undoubtedly an improvement on describing marketing as selling as it shows that marketing does encompass other activities besides selling.

As defined by Phillip Kotler marketing is —A social and managerial process by which individuals and groups obtain what they need and want through creating and exchanging products and value with others‖.

As defined by Evans & Berman —Marketing is the anticipation, management and satisfaction of demand through the exchange process‖.

Marketing is a societal process by which individuals and groups obtain what they need and want through creating, offering, and exchanging products and services of values with others." – 'Social Definition'

According to American Marketing Association "Marketing is the process of planning and executing the conception, pricing, promotion, and distribution of ideas, goods, and services to create exchanges that satisfy individual and organizational goals‖. In short Marketing is a process of:

- *Identifying Needs of the people;*
- *Making Products Accordingly; and*
- *Offering them through an Exchange Process*

Marketing Objectives

Marketing targets are a brand's characterized objectives. They layout the expectations of the advertising group, give clear bearing to colleagues to follow, and offer data for chiefs to survey and support. Promoting destinations are an essential piece of a marketing methodology. Create targets inside every one of the four P's: item, value, advancement, and spot. Under item, objectives should zero in on the deals of items and administrations.

Scope of Marketing

The extent of advertising can be perceived as far as capacities that a business person needs to perform. These incorporate the accompanying:

a. Functions of exchange: which include buying and assembling and selling?

b. Functions of physical supply: include transportation, storage and warehousing

c. Functions of facilitation: Product Planning and Development, Marketing Research, Standardizations, Grading, Packaging, Branding, Sales Promotion, Financing.

Nature of Marketing

1. Marketing is a Monetary Capacity: Marketing accepts all the business exercises engaged with getting merchandise and ventures , from the hands of makers under the control of conclusive buyers. The business ventures through which merchandise progress on their approach to conclusive buyers is the worry of advertising.

2. Promoting is a Lawful Cycle by which Possession Moves: During the time spent marketing the responsibility for moves from merchant to the buyer or from maker to the end client.

3. Advertising is an Arrangement of Associating Business Exercises: Advertising is that cycle through which a business endeavor, establishment, or association interfaces with the clients and partners with the target to acquire benefit, fulfill clients, and oversee relationship. It is the exhibition of business exercises that immediate the progression of products and enterprises from maker to customer or client.

4. Marketing is an Administrative capacity: As indicated by administrative or frameworks approach - "Marketing is the mix of exercises intended to deliver benefit through learning, making, animating, and fulfilling the necessities as well as needs of a chose fragment of the market." As per this methodology the accentuation is on how the individual association measures advertising and builds up the essential elements of marketing exercises.

5. Advertising is a social cycle: Marketing is the conveyance of a way of life to society. As per Cunningham and Cunningham (1981) cultural marketing performs three fundamental capacities:-

1. Knowing and understanding the shopper's changing requirements and needs;
2. Efficiently and adequately dealing with the organic market of items and administrations;
3. Efficient arrangement of dispersion and installment preparing frameworks.

Features of Marketing

1. **Customer-centric marketing:** Customers are the monarch for marketing firms because marketing is consumer oriented. He is at the center of all marketing decisions. The company must maintain a constant emphasis on the changing requirements and desires of its customers, as well as solutions to meet them.
2. **Marketing is a win-win situation:** Both the customer and the seller benefit from marketing. The exchange procedure allows the vendor to

sell the goods at a profit, while the buyer is able to better meet his requirements and wishes.

3. **Value-based marketing:** Only when a business tries to address the needs of the market based on a value system that is followed by the entire organisation will marketing be effective and successful.

4. **The Environment Has an Impact on Marketing:** The environment is separated into two categories: internal and external. While the internal environment can be controlled, the exterior world is uncontrollable. The political and social environment, as well as competition, technology, culture, legal, and natural environments, are all part of the external environment. Marketing operates in an external context, and as a result, it must be altered in response to changing conditions.

5. **Both for-profit and non-profit organisations benefit from marketing:** Marketing is important not only for for-profit businesses, but also for non-profit organisations such as educational institutions, temples, mosques, and hospitals.

MARKETING CONCEPT

The promoting idea holds that the way to accomplishing hierarchical objectives comprises in deciding the requirements and needs of target advertises and conveying the ideal fulfillments more viably and proficiently than contenders. Under promoting idea, the accentuation is on selling fulfillment and not simply on the selling an item. The target of advertising isn't the boost of productive deals volume, however benefits through the fulfillment of clients. The buyer is the rotate point and all promoting exercises work around this essential issue. It is, consequently, fundamental that the business visionaries recognize the clients, set up a compatibility with them, distinguish their necessities and convey the products and ventures that would meet their prerequisites. Clients give installment to an association as a trade-off for the conveyance of products and enterprises and hence structure a point of convergence for an association's promoting movement. Clients can be portrayed by numerous terms, including customer, traveler, supporter, peruser, visitor, and understudy. The phrasing can infer something about the connection between an organization and its clients, so the term _patient' infers a mindful relationship, _passenger' infers a continuous obligation regarding the wellbeing of the client, and client' suggests that the relationship is administered by a code of morals (formal or casual

The client is by and large comprehended to be the individual who settles on the choice to buy an item, as well as who pays for it. Truth be told, items are frequently purchased by one individual for utilization by another, accordingly the client and buyer need not be a similar individual. For instance, universities should showcase themselves not exclusively to planned understudies, yet additionally to their folks, vocations advocates, nearby bosses, and government financing organizations. In these conditions it very well may be hard to recognize on whom an association's advertising exertion ought to be engaged.

For some open administrations, it is society overall, and not simply the quick client, that profits by a person's utilization. On account of wellbeing administrations, society can profit by having a fit and sound populace in which the danger of getting an infectious illness is limited. Various clients inside a market have various requirements which they try to fulfill. To be completely marketing focused, an organization would need to adjust its contribution to address the issues of every person. Truth be told, not many firms can legitimize meaning to address the issues of every particular individual; all things considered, they focus on their item at an unmistakably characterized bunch in the public eye and position their item so it addresses the issues of that gathering. These subgroups are regularly alluded to as _segments'.

Self - completion Needs (Self-improvement and Acknowledgment) Regard Needs (Confidence, Acknowledgment, Status)Social Needs(Sense of having a place, love)Security Needs(Security, Protection)Physiological Needs(Food, Water, Safe house)

- **Needs, Needs and Requests**

The most essential idea fundamental marketing is that of human requirements. Purchasers are roused by their craving to fulfill complex requirements, and these ought to be the beginning stage for all promoting movement. We not, at this point live in a general public in which the primary inspiration of people is to fulfill the fundamental requirements for food and drink. Maslow (1943) perceived that, whenever people have fulfilled fundamental physiological necessities, they might be persuaded by higher-request social and self-satisfaction needs. Arranged by significance, they are physiological necessities, wellbeing needs, social requirements, regard needs and self-realization needs. Individuals will attempt to fulfill their most significant necessities first. At the point when an individual prevails with regards to fulfilling a significant need, the person in question will at that point attempt to fulfill the following - most-significant need. _Need' alludes to something that is profound established in a person's character. How people approach fulfilling that need will be molded by the social estimations of the general public to which they have a place. In certain societies the requirement for self-satisfaction might be fulfilled by a strict repentance, while different social orders may look for it through an advancement of their inventive abilities.

It is valuable to make a differentiation among requirements and needs. Needs are socially molded by the general public in which an individual lives. Needs along these lines become compelling interest for an item where there is both readiness and a capacity to pay for the item. Advertisers are constantly trying to become familiar with hidden necessities which may in the end show themselves as interest as individuals really being eager to pay cash for its items.

It should not be failed to remember that business purchasers of merchandise and ventures likewise have complex necessities which they try to fulfill when purchasing in the interest of their associations. More noteworthy multifaceted nature happens where the financial necessities of the association may not be altogether equivalent to the individual requirements of people inside the association.

Individuals have practically limitless needs, however restricted assets. They pick items that produce the most fulfillment for their cash. At the point when sponsored by purchasing power, needs become requests. Purchasers see items as groups of advantages and pick those that give then the best pack for their cash. Individuals pick the item whose advantages amount to the most fulfillment, given their needs and assets.

· **Product**

Individuals fulfill their necessities and needs with items. An item is whatever can be offered to fulfill a need or need. The idea of item isn't restricted to actual articles. Anything equipped for fulfilling a need can be known as an item. All the more extensively characterized, items incorporate encounters, people, places, associations, data, and thoughts. In this way, the term item incorporates substantially more than simply actual products or administrations. Purchasers choose which occasions to encounter, which traveler's objections to visit, which lodgings to remain in, and which eateries to belittle. To the customer these are for the most part items. Quite possibly the most intriguing zones of advertising is item arranging and advancement.

· **Value, Fulfillment and Quality**

For clients, esteem is addressed by the proportion of apparent advantages to cost paid. Clients will assess benefits as indicated by the degree to which an item permits their should be fulfilled. Clients additionally assess how well an item's advantages add to their own prosperity as contrasted and the advantages given by contenders' contributions:

Client saw esteem = Advantages getting from an item/Cost of securing the item

Customers regularly place an incentive on an item offer that is very not quite the same as the worth assumed by the provider. Business associations prevail by adding an incentive at a quicker rate than they add to their own creation costs. Worth can be added by better determining an item offer as per clients' assumptions, for instance by giving the consolation of viable after-deals administration.

Assessing clients' evaluation of significant worth isn't simple for advertisers. Division is critical to this activity, as certain gatherings of purchasers are probably going to put fundamentally higher qualities on the association's products than others. On the off chance that the cost of a decent is set too high, no deal may happen, or possibly just a coincidental deal which might be viewed by the purchaser as a _rip-off'. In the event that the cost is set too low, the provider may accomplish undeniable degrees of deals, however neglect to make any benefit on the grounds that the cost is too low to even consider taking care of its expenses. Firms need to comprehend what comprises esteem today, however how clients' view of significant worth will change over the long haul.

Consumer loyalty relies upon an item's apparent exhibition in conveying esteem comparative with a purchaser's assumptions. On the off chance that the item's presentation misses the mark regarding the client's assumptions, the purchaser is disappointed. On the off chance that exhibition matches assumptions, the purchaser is fulfilled. In the event that exhibition surpasses assumptions, the purchaser is pleased. Keen organizations plan to amuse clients by promising just what they can convey, at that point conveying more than they guarantee.

Client assumptions depend on past purchasing encounters, the assessments of companions and market data. Advertisers should be mindful so as to fix the degree of assumptions. On the off chance that they set assumptions excessively low, they may fulfill the individuals who purchase, yet neglect to pull in new clients. On the off chance that they raise assumptions excessively high, purchasers will be frustrated. Still the greater part of the present best organizations are raising assumptions and conveying execution to coordinate. These organizations reach skyward in light of the fact that they realize that clients who are only fulfilled will think that its simple to switch providers when a superior offer tags along. Along these lines, client enchant makes an enthusiastic bind to an item or administrations, not simply a levelheaded inclination, and this makes high client unwaveringness. Profoundly fulfilled clients make rehash buys, are less value touchy, remain clients longer, and talk well to others about the organization and its items. Quality straightforwardly affects item or administration execution. In this way, it is firmly connected to client worth and fulfillment. In the tightest sense, quality can be characterized as —freedom from defects‖; nonetheless, most client focused organizations go past this limited meaning of value. All things considered, quality is characterized as far as consumer loyalty.

- **Exchange**

Social orders have various manners by which they mastermind products and ventures to be obtained. In some less evolved social orders, chasing for food, or asking, might be a standard. In midway arranged economies products and ventures might be assigned to people and firms by government organizers. In current market-based economies, merchandise and ventures are gained based on trade.

ASPECTS OF MARKETING CONCEPT

The significant parts of promoting idea are:

1. **Creation of interest**: Advertising attempts to provoke interest through different methods. The makers initially learn what the clients need and afterward produce products as indicated by the requirements of the clients. There is an efficient exertion to sell products and ventures as per the necessities of the clients.

2. **Customer Direction:** Promoting includes undertaking a scope of business exercises coordinated at the formation of client fulfilling items and administrations.

3. **Integrated Marketing:** The client direction alone isn't sufficient with respect to the board. To be powerful should be supported by a fitting set up inside the country. The obligation of promoting office is to guarantee coordination of the different branches of the organization i.e., account, buy, innovative work.

4. **Profitable deals volume through consumer loyalty**: Advertising attempts to acknowledge long haul objectives of benefit, development and solidness through fulfilling clients' needs. All the fundamental exercises of an organization are intended to meet the needs of clients and as yet making sensible benefits. Present day promoting accordingly starts with the client and finishes with the client.

Importance of Marketing

Since advertising is customer arranged, it decidedly affects the business firms. It empowers the business people to improve the nature of their merchandise and enterprises. Marketing helps in improving the way of life of the individuals by offering a wide assortment of merchandise and enterprises with opportunity of decision, and by regarding the client as the main individual.

Marketing creates business both underway and in dissemination zones. Since a business firm creates income and procures benefits via doing advertising capacities, it will take part in misusing an ever increasing number of financial assets of the nation to acquire more benefits.

An enormous scope business can have its own conventional promoting network, media missions, and deals power, yet a little unit may need to rely absolutely upon individual endeavors and assets, making it casual and adaptable. Advertising represents the deciding moment a little undertaking. A venture develops, deteriorates, or perishes with the achievement or disappointment, by and large, of marketing. —Nirmal is a proper illustration of the achievement of limited scope endeavor.

Types of Marketing

a. **Goods**: Any item fabricated in mass amount, requires appropriate advertising to make it accessible to its shoppers situated in better places of the country or world. *For example*; Mobile phones manufactured in China and sold all over the world

b. **Services**: An economic activity performed to meet the consumer's demand, needs, promotion and marketing. *For example*; Ola cabs providing for local taxi services

c. **Events**: Various trade fairs, live shows, local events and other promotional events need advertising and publicity. *For example*; Indian Fashion Expo is the event where leading fashion houses participate in displaying exhibit their creation needs marketing to reach customers, manufacturers and traders.

d. **Experiences**: It even organises and customises the impression made by certain goods and services to fulfil the customer's wish. *For example*; A Europe trip package provided by makemytrip.com or tripadvisor.com

e. **Persons**: A person who wants to promote his skills, profession, art, expertise to acquire customers, take the help of marketing functions. *For example*; A chartered accountant updates his profile over linkedin.com to publicise his skills and talent to reach clients.

f. **Places**: Marketing of tourist places, cities, states and countries helps to attract visitors from all over the world. *For example*; India's Ministry of Tourism promoting India through 'Incredible India' campaign

g. **Properties**: It provides for selling of tangible and intangible properties like real estate, stocks, securities, debentures, etc. *For example*; Real estate agents publicise the residential plots to investors

h. **Organizations**: Several corporations and non-profit organisations like schools, colleges, universities, art institutes, etc. create and maintain a public impression through marketing.
For example; Circulars and advertisements made by colleges as 'admission open.'

i. **Information**: Certain information related to healthcare, technology, science, media, law, tax, market, finance, accounting, etc. have to demand among the corporate decision-makers who are marketed by some leading information agencies. *For example*; Bloomberg provides all current financial, business and market data

j. **Ideas**: Brands market their products or services through advertisements spreading a social message to connect with the consumers. *For example*; Idea 4G's advertisement spreading the message of 'sharing our real side.'

Marketing Management

We characterize marketing the executives as the craftsmanship and study of picking objective business sectors and building beneficial associations with them. This includes acquiring, holding and creating clients through making and conveying and imparting unrivaled client esteem.

In this manner, advertising the executives includes overseeing request, which thusly includes overseeing client connections.

Meaning and Definition of Marketing Management

Advertising the board is the hierarchical order which centers around the functional parts of marketing direction, procedures and strategies inside associations and on the administration of an association's promoting assets and exercises.

"Promoting the board is 'the craftsmanship and study of picking objective business sectors and getting, keeping, and developing clients through making, conveying, and imparting unrivaled client esteem' (Philip Kotler and Keller, 2008: 5)."

Marketing the executives by Philip Kotler characterizes as "the investigation, arranging, usage and control of projects intended to achieve wanted trades with target markets to accomplish hierarchical goals".

Function of Marketing Management

Function of marketing management is mentioned bellow:

- Selling
- Buying and Assembling
- Transportation
- Storage
- Standardization and Grading
- Financing
- Risk-Taking
- Market Information

Marketing Management Concepts

Marketing concepts is the philosophy that an organization should analyze the needs of their consumers and then make decisions to satisfy those needs, better than the competition.

Basically, there are five different **philosophy of marketing management** in **marketing concept** under which business enterprises conduct their marketing activity:

1. **Production Concepts:** It is one of the oldest marketing strategies in which the company emphasises the capability of its manufacturing processes. It is to make the items more affordable in order to make them available to the general public. The focus of the manufacturing concept is on number rather than product quality. The Say's Law is accompanied with a production idea that dates back to the mid-1950s. In the market, supply creates demand, according to this theory. As a result of this rule, when a corporation creates a product, it does not need to market it; it will sell itself. Because there was no technology or communications at the time, and people travelled less, the law became widely known. There used to be just one merchant in the shop, and only a few manufactures. So there used to be a limited range of things, whatever was available on the market at the time, and it would be sold. McDonald's and other fast food restaurants, for example, strive to be the best at what they do.

2. **Product Concepts:** The main goal of the product idea is to create lower-cost goods since consumers are unwilling to pay a high price for goods or services. As a result, the firms that support the product concept mass-produce the items and profit from economies of scale. When companies develop low-cost goods, they employ a broad distribution strategy in order to reach a larger audience. They can increase their productivity by increasing their market by targeting more consumers. Marketers do not value the needs and desires of customers while developing a product proposition. Their main goal is to manufacture more and more items; quantity is more important than quality. As a result, customers are frequently dissatisfied with product quality. When there were no rivals in the market, the product concept was popular; whatever you brought to the market, people would accept it. For example, Ford was the first automobile manufacturer, and it began supplying more vehicles to the market. It was the only thing available at the time, so everyone bought it.

3. **Selling Concepts:** Selling, as the name implies, is the process of promoting and selling a company's goods through large-scale marketing and promotional efforts. It makes no difference whether they meet or exceed client expectations. The goal of management in this strategy is to complete the selling transaction; they feel that once they promote their goods, their work is done. As a result, rather than forming and sustaining a long-term relationship with the consumer, the customer would return. The selling idea is a risky approach since it is founded on the faulty assumption that the corporation should sell everything it is producing rather than addressing client requests. Marketers who take this technique assume that if customers don't like a product, they'll buy something else and forget about their previous buying experience. As a result, the whole selling idea is built on the incorrect assumption that clients don't recall their previous purchasing experiences. For example, blood donations and insurance policies fall under the selling notion, in which the marketer feels their job is over after the transaction is completed.

4. **Marketing Concepts:** When it comes to marketing, the focus is on the client. It puts consumers at the center of the marketing process, identifying their needs and wants and then serving them better than the competition. In this approach, the marketer thinks that the client is always correct, and that his needs and desires should be prioritised. Here, the marketing strategy focuses on making a profit through meeting clients' requirements and wants. It promotes a straightforward strategy: instead of looking for the ideal buyers for their product, marketers should focus on creating the perfect product. As a result, marketers strive to close the gap between customers and the company's offerings. When comparing the marketing and sales concepts, you may see a significant difference between the two techniques. It is not incorrect to say that these two tactics are at different ends of the spectrum. The Coke vs. Pepsi fight is the finest example of this principle.

5. **Social marketing Concepts:** Because it analyses the marketing concept's approach, the social marketing concept's notion is focused on the welfare of the whole society. What customers require does not always imply that it will be beneficial to them in the long run. What you require and what is appropriate for you and society as a whole are two distinct concepts. We all enjoy sweet, spicy, and quick dishes, for example. When we go out, we all want the same things, but that doesn't mean it's healthy for

our health or the well-being of the entire society. The goal and purpose of the social marketing idea is to help businesses recognise that their long-term goals are significantly more essential than their short-term goals. Profit objectives Businesses should develop and operate in ways that contribute to society's long-term sustainability; businesses are a part of society and should act as such. The Coca-Cola Super Bowl Commercial 2014 "America the Beautiful." campaign is one of the greatest instances of societal marketing themes.

☙

Marketing Manager

A marketing manager is a manager in the marketing department. A marketing manager research determines, examines, and assesses demand for a product or service. They aim to increase sales by developing promotional campaigns and strategies. It's a lot of fun to promote an excellent product or service.

Marketing managers contribute directly to the success of the company in addition to assisting consumers with their concerns. This is a huge responsibility that will take a lot of effort and devotion, but it will be inspirational and influential. The task listed in the table above is extensive in scope and necessitates a wide range of skills.

Marketing managers that are successful are able to use their expertise in a range of scenarios. They may, for example, utilise their data analysis abilities to track campaign KPIs or their persuasive talents to connect with members of the media.

These are some of the most commonly cited hard and soft talents in marketing job postings:

- Budgeting
- Communication
- Collaboration
- Creativity
- Curiosity
- Analyzing data
- Empathy
- Flexibility
- Innovation

- Leadership
- Organization
- Persuasion
- Planning
- Management of a project
- Writing

Other technical or specialised abilities, such as marketing automation or search engine marketing, may be necessary depending on the function. However, regardless of their specific responsibilities, all marketing managers must be able to communicate effectively.

Marketing Management Process

Marketing Management processis a process to identifying customer needs and wants and then developing a marketing program to satisfy customer needs with a profit. So, effective marketing starts with the identification of a set of consumers and their need structure.

- **Market Analysis: Identifying customer needs**
  A marketer first analyzes and scanning the external environment to identify marketing opportunities and forecast future potential.
- **Segmentation**
  The marketing manager segments the market to identify a homogenous set of customers who are likely to respond more positively to the planned marketing program.
- **Targeting**
  Identification and selection of targeted segment(s) and positioning strategy help the marketer to develop a new product or service offered for the market.
- **Marketing Planning: Develop marketing strategies**
  After developing the product or service, The marketer also develops a strategy about coping with pricing changes in countering the competitor's counter pricing strategy.
- **Implementation of the marketing program**
  The marketing manager plans integrated marketing communication strategy through a combination of tools like advertising, sales promotion, public relations and direct marketing to promote the product or service in the market for higher consumption and brand image.

- **Control of the total marketing efforts**
  Marketing control is a process of benchmarking the expended effort and resources with the set goals.

Marketing Manager Duties and Responsibilities:
The duty of a marketing manager is to promote a company, product, or service. They ensure that the company's messaging is effective in attracting new consumers and retaining existing ones. A marketing generalist in their mid-career often fills this position. Launches, advertising, email campaigns, events, and social media are all common activities that marketing managers organise and handle. However, the particular responsibilities and operations will be determined by the company's size and structure. While a marketing manager at a smaller firm may take a "do it all" strategy, a marketing manager at a bigger company with established digital, product, or content marketing divisions may adopt a more focused approach based on the company's needs. Regardless of the sort of organization, Marketing managers must be able to create programmes and initiatives, cooperate with other departments such as product and sales, and track marketing KPIs. Marketing managers must also have a thorough awareness of the target market, target audience, and how the product or service they are advertising helps clients solve their problems. For determining how to effectively engage and sympathise with customers, market research and buyer profiles are both necessary.

The work of a marketing manager is extremely collaborative. They frequently bring together several roles (such as product marketing, digital experts, content and creative teams) to align all of the groups whose work contributes to the success of a programme or campaign. Marketing managers represent the marketing team to cross-functional groups such as product management, sales, and customer support, in addition to working directly with their marketing colleagues. They could work with these organisations to ensure that new offers are communicated in a consistent manner or to find new ways to contact customers. Outside of the organisation, some marketing managers cultivate relationships. Strong connections with vendors, partners, and members of the media are critical for spotting chances to raise product awareness and better engage the company's target audience. A marketing manager, for example, may need to communicate with a third-party firm developing an advertising campaign or reach out to members of the press for assistance in promoting a new product.

Marketing managers are also in charge of keeping senior management up to date on the status of marketing efforts and reporting on campaign results. While a marketing manager in a major firm normally reports to the director or vice president of marketing, in a smaller company, the CMO or CEO may report directly to the marketing manager.

- Planning For Future
- Advising the Top Management
- Selection and Placement of Salesmen
- Training the Sales Force
- Compensating the Sales Personnel
- Organising the sales organisation
- Direction and Co-Ordination
- Controlling the Activities of Employees
- Designing Viable Sales Policy
- Meet Challenging Tasks

Important Questions:

1. Define Market
2. Define marketing management
3. Define the terms Exchange
4. What is marketing?
5. Explain scope, objectives and types of marketing?
6. List down the importance of marketing?
7. Explain marketing concepts.
8. What are the features of marketing?
9. What is marketing management? Explain the different concepts of marketing?
10. Explain the aspects of marketing concepts.
11. List down the function of marketing management.
12. Who is marketing manager?
13. Discuss the duties and responsibilities of Marketing Manger
14. Explain the marketing manager process.
15. Define Production Concept

16. Define Product Concept
17. Brief 'Selling Concept"
18. Write short notes on: a) Targeting b) Integrated Marketing c) Segmentation

II
Market & Buyer

Functions of Marketing

Marketing isn't simply auctioning off merchandise and enterprises to the clients; it implies much more than that.It begins with the investigation of the possible market, to item improvement, to piece of the overall industry catching, to keep up warm relations with the clients.

1. **Function of Exchange:**

- **Buying:** Purchasing is the initial phase during the time spent promoting. It includes what to purchase, what quality, how much, from whom, when and at, what cost. Individuals in business purchase to build deals or to diminish costs. Buying specialists are quite affected by quality, administration, and cost. The items that the retailers purchase for resale are controlled by the need and inclinations of theirs. clients.

- **Selling:** To connect with the shoppers spread over an immense topographical region, selling and dissemination channels are to be chosen admirably. . It is center of Marketing. It is worried about the forthcoming purchasers to really finish the acquisition of an article. It includes move of responsibility for to the purchaser. Selling has a significant influence in understanding a definitive point of hoop benefit. Selling is upgraded by methods for individual selling, publicizing, exposure and deals advancement. Viability and effectiveness in selling decides the volume of organization's benefits and productivity.

2. Functions of Physical Supply

- **Assembling:** In the wake of purchasing all the material buy ought to be gathered at the focal spot, it is called collecting. Collecting intends to buy fundamental segment parts and to fit them together to make an item. 'Sequential construction system' demonstrates a creation line comprised of absolutely gathering activities. The gathering activity includes the appearance of individual segment parts at the work spot and giving of these parts to be affixed together as a get together or sub-get together.

  Sequential construction system is a game plan of laborers and machines where every individual has a specific work and the work is passed straightforwardly starting with one specialist then onto the next until the item is finished. Then again, 'creation lines' infers a creation line comprised of tasks that structure or change the physical or once in a while compound attributes of the item in question. Gathering is needed for all sort of item whether they are horticultural items, purchaser item or modern item.

- **Transport and handling:** Transportation implies are chosen for move of the merchandise from the assembling units to the wholesalers, retailers and shoppers. Transportation is the actual methods by which products are moved from where they are created to where they are required for utilization. It makes place, utility. Transportation is fundamental from the acquisition of crude material to the conveyance of completed items to the client's places. Advertising depends primarily on railways, trucks, streams, pipelines and air transport.

  The kind of transportation is picked on a few contemplations, for example, reasonableness, speed and cost. Transportation might be performed either by the purchaser or by the vender. The nature and sort of the transportation offices decide the degree of the promoting territory, the routineness in stock, uniform value upkeep and simple admittance to the provider or dealer.

- **Storage and Warehousing:** The merchandise are for the most part created in masses and thusly should be put away in stockrooms prior to being sold in the market in little amounts. It includes holding of merchandise in appropriate (i.e., usable or saleable) condition from the time they are delivered until they are required by clients (in the event of completed items) or by the creation division (if there should be an occurrence of crude materials and stores); putting away shields the products from disintegration and helps in persisting excess for future utilization or use underway.

Products might be put away in different distribution centers arranged at better places, which is prominently known as warehousing. Stockrooms ought to be arranged at such places from where the dissemination of merchandise might be simpler and less expensive. Circumstance of stockrooms is likewise significant from the perspective on brief taking care of crisis requests. Putting away accepts significance when creation is territorial or utilization might be provincial. Retail firms are designated "stores".

- **Processing andpackaging:** Bundling and Marking: To make the item more appealing and self-useful, it is stuffed and named rattling off the fixings utilized, item use, producing subtleties, expiry date, and so on.

3. Facilitating functions

- **Marketing Finance:** It includes the employments of money to meet monetary necessity of organizations managing the different exercises of promoting. The administrations to give the credit and cash required, the expenses of getting stock under the control of the last client is regularly alluded to as money work in Marketing. Account is as fundamental in Marketing as underway of merchandise or administrations. Course of action of sufficient account ought to be made to deal with any issue emerged from vulnerability of cost, from credit deal, and so on.

  In advertising, accounts are required for working capital and fixed capital which might be made sure about from three sources—possessed capital, bank advances and advance and exchange credit. (Given by makers to distributer and by the distributer to the retailers.) as such; different sorts of funds are transient account, medium-term money, and long haul money.

- **Marketing risk-bearing:** Marketing taking is the other significant encouraging elements of Marketing. Business firms or business visionaries should face different challenges over the span of advertising. Burglary, cheating, strike, lock-up, battle, over weight of advance, social assistance, disease, hurt, mishap and so forth may make individual powerlessness welcoming surprising occasions in future. Marketing implies misfortune because of some unexpected conditions in future.

Marketing bearing in promoting alludes to the monetary Marketing interest in the responsibility for held for a foreseen request including the potential misfortunes because of a fall in costs and the misfortunes from waste, devaluation, outdated nature, fire and floods or whatever other misfortune that may happen with the entry of time.Accident may occur while shipping products starting with one spot then onto the next. Nature of the merchandise may decay causing decrease in cost or costs may change. Such occasions unfavorably influence the business firms and business people. From creation of products to its selling stage, numerous Marketings are included because of changes in economic situations, normal causes and human components. Changes in design or innovations likewise cause hazards. Administrative proportions of government may likewise cause hazards. Marketings may emerge throughout transportation.

They may likewise be because of rot, disintegration and mishaps, or because of variance in the costs brought about by changes in their market interest. The different Marketings are generally named as spot hazard, time hazard and actual Marketing, and so forth

- **Standardization:** Different exercises that encourage Marketing are normalization and reviewing. Normalization implies foundation of specific principles or particulars for items dependent on characteristic actual characteristics of any ware.

  This may include amount (weight or size) or it might include quality (shading, shape, appearance, material, taste, pleasantness and so on) Government may likewise set a few norms, for instance, in the event of farming items. A standard passes on a consistency of the items.

- **Grading:** The item is evaluated according to its quality and the nature of its crude materials. Evaluating implies characterization of normalized items into certain very much characterized classes or gatherings. It includes the division of items into classes made of units having comparative attributes of size and quality. Evaluating is vital for crude materials, Marketing of agrarian items, (for example, foods grown from the ground), mining items, (for example, coal, iron and manganese) and woodland items, (for example, lumber). Marked buyer items may bear grade names A, B, C.

- **Market information:** The significance of this encouraging capacity of Marketing has been perceived as of late. The solitary sound establishment on which Marketing choices might be based is right and convenient market data. Right realities and data diminish the previously mentioned chances and in this way bring about expense decrease. Current advertising requires a ton of data enough, precisely and expediently. Promoting data makes a vender realize when to sell, at what cost to sell, who are the contenders, and so forth Marketing data and its appropriate investigation has prompted advertising research which has now become a free part of promoting. To recognize the necessities, needs and requests of the shoppers and afterward examining the distinguished data to show up at different choices for the fruitful advertising of a company's items and administrations.

  Business firms gather, examine and decipher realities and data from inside sources, for example, records, sales reps and discoveries of the statistical surveying office. They additionally look for realities and data from outside sources, for example, business distributions, government reports and business research firms.

  Retailers need to think about causes of supply and furthermore about clients "purchasing intentions and purchasing propensities". Producers need to think about retailers and about publicizing media. Firms in both these gatherings need data about 'contender' exercises and about their business sectors.

  Indeed, even extreme customers need market data about accessibility of items, their quality norms, their costs and furthermore about the after deal administration office. Regular hotspots for buyers are salesmen, media notices, associates, and so on.

- **Demand and supply creation:** This incorporates all endeavors of merchants to initiate purchasers to buy their items. To build deals, request creational endeavors like individual selling, publicizing, and so forth are embraced by vender.

- **Market research:** A total examination on contenders, shopper assumptions and request is done prior to dispatching an item into the market.

4. Other Functions

- **Identifying market opportunities**: An appropriate arrangement is planned dependent on the objective clients, piece of the overall industry to be caught and the degree of creation conceivable.

  Promoting products and services: In light of the examination information, the item or administration configuration is made. Subsequent stage is to make individuals mindful of the item or administration through ads.

- **Strategic Marketing Planning**: Vital arranging includes building up a procedure to meet rivalry and guarantee long haul endurance and development. The advertising capacity assumes a significant part in this cycle and it gives data and different contributions to help in the readiness of the association's essential arrangement.

Buyer Behaviour

When establishing the marketing mix, a company that wants to be successful must consider buyer behaviour. The acts consumers perform when buying and using things are referred to as buyer behaviour. Marketers must understand customer behaviour, such as how changing the price of a product affects the buyer's impression of the product and, as a result, sales, or how a certain review on social media might change the marketing mix totally based on the target market's remarks (buyer behavior/input).

Marketers must understand how clients make purchasing decisions in order to comprehend buyer behaviour. Consumers and corporations both use systems to make purchasing decisions. Cultural, social, individual, and psychological aspects influence these decision-making processes. The consumer decision-making process is divided into numerous parts, as indicated in the diagram (Figure).

The Purchase Decision-Making Process of Consumers

Step 1 - Need Recognition

Step 2 - Information Search

Step 3 - Evaluation of alternatives

Step 4 - Purchase

Step 5 - Post-Purchase behaviour

The process begins with the recognition of a need. It might be as easy as running out of coffee to trigger a need for acknowledgment. Need recognition can also happen over time, such as when a consumer's decision to buy a new car is influenced by recurrent car repairs. (See (Figure) for the first step.) The buyer then obtains information. If a consumer is considering buying a home, he or she may conduct research on financing, available homes, styles, and locations, among other things (Step 2). Once the consumer has obtained the necessary information, he or she must weigh the many options available (Step 3). A consumer might, for example, rule out any residences that cost more than $150,000 or It takes more than 30 minutes to go to work. The consumer will make a decision based on the options after they have been evaluated. The consumer then makes a purchasing decision, whether to buy or not to buy (Step 4). Finally, the customer evaluates the decision and his or her pleasure with the purchase, which includes not just the home but also the buying process (Step 5).

Consumer Decision-Making Influences

From the moment a person perceives a need to post-purchase behaviour, cultural, social, individual, and psychological aspects influence consumer decision-making. We'll go through each of these points in further depth. It's critical to comprehend the significance of these factors in consumer decision-making.

Culture

Culture has an impact on purchase positions within the family. Culture refers to the set of values, beliefs, attitudes, and symbols that have been developed to influence human behaviour. Culture refers to a group of people's habits and traditions as manifested in their art, food, costumes/clothing, architecture, and language, as well as other distinctive expressions of a group of related persons. Culture is concerned with the environment. Finland's nomads, for example, have created an Arctic survival culture. Similarly, the indigenous peoples of the Brazilian jungle have developed a culture that is suited to jungle life.

Culture is, by definition, a social phenomenon. Human interaction is what establishes values and defines acceptable behaviour. Culture creates a sense of order in society by establishing common expectations. These expectations are sometimes formalised into legislation; for example, you must stop your car when approaching a red light. In certain cultures, a young man's transition from youth to manhood is marked by a specific rite of passage (such as a bar mitzvah in Jewish culture). Young women have a rite of passage in some cultures, but young males do not (such as a quinceaera in Hispanic culture). A value or belief will stay part of the culture as long as it meets the demands of society. When something is no longer useful, its worth or belief diminishes. For A majority of Americans, for example, no longer believe that excessively big families are "excellent." This is due to the fact that most Americans now live in cities rather than rural areas, and children are no longer required to conduct farm chores.

Social Factors

Most consumers are likely to seek out the opinions of others to reduce their search and evaluation effort or uncertainty, especially as the perceived risk of the decision increases. Consumers may also seek out others' opinions for guidance on new products or services, products with image-related attributes, or products where attribute information is lacking or uninformative. Specifically, consumers interact socially with reference groups, opinion leaders, and family members to obtain product information and decision approval. All the formal and informal groups that influence the buying behavior of an individual are considered that person's reference groups. Consumers may use products or brands to identify with or become a member of a group. They learn from observing how members of their reference groups consume, and they use the same criteria to make their own consumer decisions. A reference group might be a fraternity or sorority, a group you work with, or a club to which you belong.

Individual Factors

Personal qualities unique to each individual, such as gender and personality, impact a person's purchasing decisions. Individual qualities tend to remain consistent throughout one's life. For example, most people do not change their gender, and changing one's personality necessitates a total life reorientation.

Men and women have varied needs in terms of health and aesthetic items due to physiological variations. Men and women play different cultural, social, and economic roles, and these differences have an impact on their decision-making processes. Men and women shop in different ways. According to studies, men and women have similar shopping goals, such as wanting reasonable prices, high-quality items, and a pleasant shopping experience. They may enjoy shopping in a nice, low-pressure environment, but they may not feel the same way about shopping in general. The majority of women enjoy shopping, while their male counterparts claim to despise it and only shop when they have to. Men also prefer uncomplicated shopping experiences, stores with fewer options, and convenience. Gender inequalities persist when it comes to internet buying. According to recent studies, women prefer to purchase for future needs, whilst men prefer to shop for urgent needs. Furthermore, women are more likely than males to make impulse purchases, whilst men are more likely to consider logically before making purchases.

Every customer has an own personality. Personality is a wide notion that may be thought of as a way of arranging and grouping how a person reacts to stimuli on a regular basis. As a result, personality is made up of both psychological and environmental factors. It encompasses people's basic inclinations, particularly their most prominent traits. Despite the fact that personality is one of the least relevant notions in the study of consumer behaviour, some marketers believe it has an impact on the types and brands of items bought. A consumer's choice of car, clothing, or jewellery, for example, may represent one or more personality traits.

Psychological Factors

Psychological elements such as perception, beliefs, and attitudes also influence a person's purchasing decisions. Consumers use these factors to engage with their environment. They are the instruments that customers use to perceive their emotions, collect and analyse data, generate thoughts and views, and take action. Psychological factors, unlike the other three influences on consumer behaviour, can be influenced by a person's surroundings because they are used on specific occasions. Individuals, for example, will perceive and process stimuli differently depending on whether they are sitting in class concentrating on an instructor's lecture, sitting outside of class conversing to friends, or sitting at home watching television.

B2B Purchase Decision-Making

Buyer Behavior and Business Marketplaces in B2B Purchase Decision-Making Business-to-business (B2B) buyer behaviour and business markets are distinct from consumer markets. Institutions such as hospitals and schools, as well as manufacturers, wholesalers, and retailers, as well as various parts of government, are all part of the business market. The intended use is the main distinction between a consumer and a corporate product. For example, if a consumer buys a specific brand of computer for home use, it is classified as a consumer good. It is considered a business good if a Netflix purchasing agent purchases the exact same machine for a Netflix scriptwriter. Why? The reason for this is because Netflix is a company, so the computer will be utilised in a corporate setting.

The Process of Making a Decision

Organizational purchases frequently carry a higher level of risk than individual consumer purchases. As a result, businesses (and other organisations) tend to base purchase decisions on greater data and logical decision-making, ensuring that purchases maximise value for the company while minimising risk. As a result, the procedure of making a corporate purchase differs from that of a consumer. The procedures are similar: recognising the requirement, establishing specifications, doing an information search (including supplier identification), evaluating (including supplier evaluation), purchasing ("go or no-go"), and post-purchase evaluation. The main distinction between the two processes is that businesses decide ahead of time what exactly they need (specifying requirements) and then look for items that fulfil those requirements. As a result, the purchases are more likely to meet the needs of the entire company, lowering the risk.

The B2B Market's Characteristics

The following are the main distinctions between consumer and business markets:

1. **Purchase volume:** Business clients buy in far larger quantities than consumers. To create one day's worth of M&Ms, Mars needs to buy many truckloads of sugar. Every day, Home Depot purchases hundreds of batteries for resale to customers. Every day, the federal government must use (and buy) millions of pens.

2. **Customer base:** Business marketers typically have a smaller customer base than consumer marketers. As a result, it's considerably easier to spot potential purchasers and keep track of existing requirements. Because there are more than 125 million consumer households in the United States, there are considerably fewer clients for aeroplanes or industrial crane businesses than there are for consumer products companies The United States of America

3. **Buyers' locations:** Business customers are substantially more concentrated geographically than consumers. Silicon Valley and a few other places are home to the computer industry. Seattle, Washington, St. Louis, Missouri, and Dallas/Fort Worth, Texas are all known for their aircraft production. Suppliers to major manufacturers frequently locate near them to reduce distribution costs and improve communication.

4. **Direct Distribution:** Because such sales usually involve big volumes or custom-built items such as heavy machinery, business sales are frequently made directly to the buyer. Intermediaries such as

wholesalers and retailers are more likely to sell consumer goods.

Consumers and Organizations make Buying Decisions

Buyer behaviour refers to the actions that consumers and businesses take in order to purchase and use goods. Recognizing a need, seeking information, assessing alternatives, purchasing the product, appraising the purchase outcome, and engaging in post-purchase behaviour are all steps in the consumer purchase decision-making process. The process is influenced by a number of things. Consumer decision-making is influenced by cultural, societal, individual, and psychological aspects. The steps in the business buy decision-making model are need recognition, specification setting, information search, alternative evaluation versus requirements, purchase, and post-purchase behaviour. Buying volume, number of customers, buyer location, direct distribution, and rational purchase decisions are the primary differences between consumer and commercial markets. Marketing research is the process of planning, gathering, and analysing data to understand more about a company's target market, as well as collecting and evaluating data important to marketing decisions.

Buying Motives

There is always a buying purpose behind every sale, but it is never simply to own the item in issue. On the other side, prospects are always under the impression that owning the object will fulfil some specific want. A motivation is the internal state that drives or motivates someone to take action.

In the words of W. J. Stanton, "A motive may be defined as a drive or an urge for which can individual seeks satisfaction. It becomes a buying motive when the individual seeks satisfaction through the purchase of something."

Some important definitions of motive are as under

In the words of D. J. Durdian, *"Buying motives are those influences or considerations which provide the impulse to buy, induce action or determine choice in the purchase of goods and services."*

According to Dr. R.S. Davar – *"A motive is defined as an inner urge that moves or prompts a person to action."*

According to Berelson and Steiner – *"A motive is the inner state that energizes, activates or moves and that directs or channels behaviour to work goals."*

Classification of Buying Motives:

1. **Purchasing Motives: Physical, Psychological, and Sociological:** The psychological buying impulses are linked to the satisfying of basic human necessities for survival, such as food, shelter, and clothing, as well as security. The drive for prestige or self-preservation, for example, is one of the psychological buying impulses. The sociological purchasing reasons are linked to current motives and are expected in all social circumstances.

2. **Learned and Inherent Purchasing Motives:** Acquired purchasing motives are learned motives that are impacted by environmental variables. Economy, information, labour efficiency, profit facility, quality, beauty, fashion, social influence, acceptability, and other factors are all tied to socioeconomic conditions and educational levels. A person's intrinsic buying incentives are there from birth. It stems from primal human inclinations, whereas developed purchasing motivations are focused with the surroundings. Hunger, thirst, sleep, relaxation, security, and playing amusement all have an impact on them.

3. **Buying Motives: Primary and Selective:**
The key purchasing impulses raise overall product demand rather than specific desire for a certain product or brand. This group of primary motives includes the demand for radios, televisions, automobiles, motorcycles, and other such items. Selective purchasing reasons drive the demand for specific brands, such as Bajaj's Chetak Scooter, Onida TV, Philips Radios, and so on.

4. **Buying Motives, Aware and Unaware:**
The conscious buying motives are those that the buyer can identify without the assistance of marketing functions such as advertising, personal selling, or promotional instruments. The satisfaction of a customer's current demands is influenced by conscious buying intentions. Such purchasing incentives are formed in the customers' subconscious brains and are unaffected by external environmental influences. Dormant buying motives are silent reasons that do not impact purchasers unless the marketing functions draw their attention to them. As a result, dormant purchase impulses are linked to the satisfying of requirements established by marketing functions. Without the persuasion of marketing activities, a consumer would be unaware of such needs.

5. **Emotional and Rational Buying Motives:**
Alfred Gross divided buying motives into two categories: emotional and

rational.

A client makes reasonable or cost-effective purchasing selections in order to obtain at least a couple of the following benefits:

a. Where it is more lucrative to buy.
b. Where there is a time savings.
c. In cases where the items are comparable or uniform.
d. Where the item is straightforward to use (v) Where the thing has multiple applications.
e. When it comes to storing the product, it saves room.
f. When there is a cost-cutting strategy in place.
g. If the product is well-designed.
h. When compared to other products, it is a superior product.
i. Where the product is long-lasting and the consumer has faith in it.
j. Where the merchandise may be found easily

Buying Motives for Products and Patronage:
Product purchasing incentives drive a person to purchase a particular item. The physical and psychological characteristics of the goods, such as design, colour, size, package, quality, and price, all contribute to this drive.
A person's decision to buy a product from a specific merchant, dealer, or producer is influenced by the patronage motive. If a customer is satisfied with a seller's/product, producer's he prefers to buy that seller's/products producer's because of certain benefits, such as home delivery of purchased goods, a reasonable price, the seller's/location, shop's the assortment of goods, goodwill demonstration of the product and shop decoration, and the seller's/good producer's behaviour.

Importance of Knowing Buying Motives of Customers:
Knowing what motivates clients to buy is crucial for the following reasons:

1. Salesmanship success - A salesperson can succeed by learning more about the buying motivations of customers. The salesman will be able to make goods and services available to the customer's choice in price, quality, and other requirements based on a fundamental understanding of buying motives. Customers are satisfied in a short length of time in this manner.

2. Aids product planning - Knowing customers' purchasing motivations aids product planning by applying proper colour, design, size, package, pricing, and other factors to the product in accordance with consumer preferences.

3. Helps with product price - Understanding the buyer's motivations can also help with product pricing. Customer with a strong emotional attachment may be willing to pay a greater price, whereas a knowing consumer will only be willing to pay a fair amount.

4. Aids in the creation of promotional materials - Every sales organisation takes efforts to promote sales through promotional strategies such as advertising, sales promotion, personal selling, and publicity. The marketing manager will be able to select appropriate promotional tactics to more effectively induce his clients if he knows what motivates them to buy.

5. Makes it easier to choose distribution channels — Many clients are affected by "self-protective" purchasing reasons and prefer to buy from wholesalers. This could be owing to the services provided by middlemen to their clients. In this case, the producer must consider the buyer's motivations.

6. Building goodwill - By studying the behaviours of the clients, any seller or trader may satisfy them. Customers develop brand loyalty for specific manufacturers' items. Consumer behaviour is what builds a company's and its products' goodwill.

7. Efforts to change a customer's buying motivations - Efforts can be made to change a customer's motives by learning from his buying reasons. Certain buyers may prefer to acquire things from that merchant only if the seller's behaviour is excellent. before settling on the most acceptable distribution channels.

Types of Buying Motives:

1. **Utility:** Everyone wants to get the most out of their limited resources. As a result, a seller must have awareness about purchasing reasons of utility. The success of a seller is determined by the amount of time spent establishing the element of utility in the types of buyers. The item is purchased in proportion to the utility element's influence.

2. **Fear:** Fear is a negative motive that has a lot of force. There are various types of fear. For instance, dread of death, fear of loss, and so forth. Fear aids in the sale of any item. After doing a thorough investigation into the reasons for the fear, a seller should implement sales promotion, advertisement, and other techniques. For example, a man purchases an insurance policy because he is afraid of dying. Because they are afraid

of theft or fire, traders insure their store or factory. Fear is a powerful motivator in the sale of any product. These examples demonstrate that the primary incentives for purchase are self-defense and the protection of others.

3. **Money Desire:** Almost everyone is motivated to earn money and save money. It is for this reason that every producer aims to maximise profit by lowering costs. The only desire to make money has kept dealers, producers, salaried class, and others busy at all hours of the day and night. A seller who has this desire can only make money. He has the ability to produc "Buy the Bata shoe and save money," he said in a plea to the public. "Buy Tata washing powder and save money," says a Khaitan enthusiast, referring to a profit bargain, for example. He makes an effort to sell his merchandise by igniting people's desire through these commercials.

4. **Love or Affection:** The feelings of love and affection touch everyone. The person purchases various items based on the purpose of love and affection. For example, a guy may be motivated to purchase a lovely saree for his wife, while parents may be motivated to purchase sweets, clothing, and toys for their children. This motive allows a merchant to sell his items.

5. **Pride:** Some people are found with pride. Envy is a common emotion in people. the females Everyone loves to hear his phoney flattery. After satisfying his or her ego, the buyer is willing to spend a higher price for the items. As a result, a vendor should be aware of the pride motive.

6. **Fashion:** We are living in the age of fashion. Every shopper makes an attempt to purchase things that are trendy at the time. Fashion is the urge to follow in the footsteps of others. Everybody wants to win the fashion race that is currently taking place. As a result, an effective seller should be aware of this motivation as well. Consider the DCM commercial.

7. **Health:** Everyone strives to improve his or her health. This health-related motivation motivates the man to purchase the things. Vitamin pills, for example, or a a healthy diet and tonic, for example This motive is more essential in the situation of children.

8. **Comfort and Convenience:** Everyone wishes to live in a comfortable and convenient environment. People buy products related to comfort and pleasures because of this motivation. Fans, washing machines, scooters, coolers, and automobiles, for example.

9. **Sex:** A vendor is obliged to engage himself in the purchasing impulses for sex-related things. The purchase motive connected to sex plays a significant role in the selling of a variety of items. If there is no purchasing motivation for sex, the fashion style may be discontinued. Both men and women purchase a variety of products in order to achieve their goals. They are attracted to one other. The merchant can take advantage of the sex-related purpose and sell these things in bulk. In the present age of advertising, it's worth noting that sex has taken precedence.

10. **Possession:** Everyone has a natural desire to keep the things that are in their possession. This motivation drives him to purchase a house, a car, and other items.Curiosity is a key reason, and it is curiosity that inspires a large number of tourists to travel and view places of interest, as well as making new goals possible. This motivates shoppers to purchase a variety of items on a daily basis. Several publishers are releasing books, novellas, and plays in order to pique readers' interest.

Important Questions:

1. Explain the functions of Exchange
2. Explain the functions of Physical distribution
3. Explain the Facilitating function
4. Write short notes on buying, selling and assembling
5. Write short notes on transport, Market information and warehousing
6. Write short notes on financing, risk taking and after sales service
7. Define the terms Exchange
8. How do consumers and organizations make buying decisions?
9. Explain the consumer purchase decision-making process.
10. Explain the differences between the business purchase decision-making process and the consumer purchase decision-making process.
11. How do business markets differ from consumer markets?
12. How do consumers and organizations make buying decisions?
13. What is known as buying motives define it?
14. List down the classification of buying motives?
15. Explain the Importance of Knowing Buying Motives of Customers.
16. Elaborate the types of buying motives.

III

Distribution Channel

SELECTION OF DISTRIBUTION CHANNEL

For any assembling association, the achievement of its item in the commercial center relies upon how well it is made accessible to its last purchasers. Dispersion channels assume a vital part in this movement. The channel accomplices are likewise called mediators; in light of the job they play to carry the organization nearer to its clients. The organization should set up solid conveyance channel to make the items or administrations accessible to its clients and to produce more grounded associations with them. For any assembling association, the achievement of its item in the commercial center relies upon how well it is made accessible to its last customers. Appropriation channels assume a vital part in this action. The channel accomplices are additionally called middle people, due to the job they play to carry the organization nearer to its clients. The organization should set up solid conveyance channel to make the items or administrations accessible to its clients and to produce more grounded associations with them.

The dissemination channel expands cost to the organization, however it additionally assumes a tremendous and significant part in making the organization's items accessible in the regions where they can be purchased by the clients quick. Without a proper appropriation channel, all the advancement endeavors (for example publicizing, selling and so forth) will fizzle, on the grounds that the interest created by such endeavors won't be satisfied if our items are not made accessible on the lookout.

In the event of administrations likewise, the dispersion channel networks have an essential influence. (For example telecom, protection, common assets and so on) To fabricate solid associations with its clients, the organization should likewise focus on form similarly more grounded relationship with its channel accomplices. A powerless channel can't assemble or uphold a solid client base. These channel accomplices help the organization in the execution of many showcasing activities locally.

Alongside supporting the organization with improved clients contact and administration, circulation channel additionally can give entirely significant market data about the patterns in the business, customer inclinations and rivalry exercises. This data can be valuable to the organization in forming its own promoting procedure and strategies.

In the event that an organization sells through its dissemination channel, the organization's business association should be adjusted to help the channel. These wholesalers or vendors might be selective channel accomplices of our items or they might be disseminating other contenders' items too. Both require distinctive kind of taking care of.

Channel of Distribution refers to the chain of businesses or intermediaries through which a good or service passes until it reaches the end consumer. A distribution channel can include wholesalers, retailers, distributors and even the internet.

According to Philip Kotler – "Every producer seeks to link together the set of marketing intermediaries is called the marketing Channel also Trade Channel or Channel of Distribution".

According to Mc Carthy – "Any sequence of institution from the producer to the consumer including one or any number of middlemen is called Channel of Distribution".

According to Morris and Sirgy (1985), the channel members alter their functions and adjust their organizations and programmes to cope with the changing environment. Therefore, the evolution of a channel system is an ongoing adaptation of organizations to economic, technological, and socio-political forces both within the channel and in the external environment.

Direct and indirect channels of distributions can be further categorized as follows:

1. Zero-Level Channel:

Zero-level channel is the most direct, shortest, cost-effective and simplest channel wherein products/services are directly sold by the producers to their respective customers without involvement of intermediaries i.e., wholesalers and retailers. Produces have full control over the distribution process and can sell these products by door-to-door sales, direct mail or through their own retail stores (physical and /or online).

2. One-Level Channel:

This distribution channel involves only one intermediary i.e., retailer. A producer sells their products / services through big retailers who in turn sell it to the final or end-consumer. This channel reduces the cost of selling goods to the end customer and is often suited for distribution of consumer durables and high-valued products.

3. Two-Level Channel:

This distribution channel involves two intermediaries i.e., wholesaler and retailer. As the most commonly used and traditional distribution process, this channel involves a wholesaler who purchases products from the producer and sells it to the retailers. The retailers sell the product (possibly along with many other products) to the final or end-consumer.

4. Three-Level Channel:

The three-level channel involves three intermediaries i.e., agent, wholesaler and retailer. A producer who would prefer to offload the cost of distribution sells his products to selling agents. These agents distribute the product among few wholesalers and each of them distributes the products across many retailers reaching out to many end-consumers. This channel is suitable for wider distribution of various industrial and agricultural produce.

Important Functions of Distribution Channels

Distribution channels have various significant functions that affect the workings of the producers of products / services.

These functions are discussed as follows:

1. Sorting:

Distribution channels can sort out large heterogeneous products produced by businesses into smaller and manageable homogenous units (i.e., according to quality, size and price). They aim at ensuring that varieties of products produced in large amounts are eventually converted into products / services consumed by their customers at targeted markets across different locations.

2. Accumulation:

Accumulation is a significant function of distribution channels which involves recognising changes in demand for products/services across several markets. Accordingly, these channels accumulate inventories and/or unsold products to maintain quality and price stability in the market.

3. Assorting:

Distributors also assort various products by collecting different products in small volumes for retail distribution. Assorting by distributors directly caters to customers wants for variety of products but in small volume. For example, shampoos, toothpaste, soaps, detergents, etc., are produced in bulk but assorted in retail shops in small volumes for customers.

4. Allocation/Packing:

The assorted products are again allocated into smaller packages and distributed to customers across different regions depending upon the demand for the assorted products.

5. Promotion:

As they have an advantage of being in proximity to the demand and supply forces of the market they can strategically contact and promote the products to the end-customers. Depending on the product, distribution channels can promote through special displays, sale or discount prices, inclusion in advertisements on television, Internet, etc.

6. Negotiation:

Negotiation among distribution channels is a unique way of maintaining relationships between vendors, distributors and producers. Relationships are maintained by mutually acceptable rules on pricing (tariffs), delivery time and methods, payment methods and schedules to avoid conflicts and maintain cost-effective costs of distribution.

7. Risk Taking:

Distribution channels undertake risks by making advance payments to producers for products that have not been sold to customers. They undertake risks associated with possible damage during transportation, assortment, packaging, possibility of low demand, shortages in supply, etc. for products.

Factors affecting choice of channels include:

1. Product-Related Factors:

Product-related factors for selecting choice of channels are associated with the characteristics of product like durability, tangibility, use or utility, etc.

Some considerations are discussed below:

(a) Value of the product – A highly expensive products like premium watches, gold jewellery, etc., will use a small distribution channel, while relative inexpensive products like readymade garments, soaps, etc. may use a longer distribution channel.

(b) Standardised or customised product – Standardised products have uniform characteristics and can be produced in bulk, and can require a long distribution channel. Customised products are custom-made as per customer needs and will require a direct-sales approach channel than standardised products.

(c) Perishability – Perishability in marketing is related to products which can be easily stored for distribution at any time frame. Fruits and vegetables are highly perishable and usually have a short distribution channel while durables like FMCG goods (shampoos, soaps, body deodorants, etc.) have a longer distribution channel.

(d) Technical nature – Products that are technical in nature and bulkier than most consumer durables would require a distribution channel that is closer to the customers. For example, refrigerators, automobiles, etc.

2. Company-Related Factors:

Company-related factors are related to the internal environment in which a business operates:

(a) Goodwill – A business that experiences a good reputation will not necessarily involve middlemen.

(b) Controlling distribution – Businesses that control distribution either to control costs, quality or pricing products do not rely on middlemen.

(c) Financial strength – Businesses with strong financial base can develop their own channels of distribution. However, businesses with weaker financial base usually rely on middle-men.

3. Competitive Factors:

The nature and extent of competition also determines the choice of channels. Producers may either imitate their competitors and use middlemen or rely on direct-sales to show a competitive edge over their competitors.

4. Market-Related Factors:

Market-related factors are associated with the characteristics of the relevant target customers.

(a) Number of buyers – Markets with large number of buyers will require the involvement of intermediaries to reach out to all the customers.

(b) Types of buyers – If there are more buyers to purchase goods that are widely available items then middlemen can get involved. However, buyers purchased specialised goods like industrial products or premium products then direct- customer trading is a convenient option.

(c) Buying quantity – Products which are purchased in smaller quantities require the involvement of middlemen.

(d) Size of the market – If the market area is scattered across regions, then the producers should consider middlemen for distribution.

5. Environmental Factors:

Environmental factors are associated with the surrounding external environment in which a business operates.

(a) Economic conditions – Economic conditions which reflect stability like low inflation, higher incomes, etc. can lead producers to have longer distribution channels. During economic slowdowns like higher inflation, high interest rates, etc. the length of distribution channels can be reduced.

(b) Legal restrictions – Legislative restrictions can determine the choice and extent of distributions channels for producers. For example, the Monopolies Restrictive Trade Practice (MRTP) Act restricts businesses from monopoly in supply and distribution of products or controlling production and prices of distribution.

(c) Competitors' channels – Businesses prefer to imitate their competitors' approach of distribution to avoid risks of higher costs of distribution.

(d) Fiscal structure – Fiscal structure of a country reflects the structure of taxes and the overall financial size of the government that can possibly fuel economic growth. Fiscal structures across states may vary and accordingly affect the costs of distribution.

Distribution Channels – Systems

By convention channel of distribution included only merchant middlemen, agents and brokers. Facilitating agencies such as banks, common carriers, advertising agencies, warehousing companies were excluded from the channel concept as these would not take title to or negotiate the purchase and sale of products.

Under the systems approach the channel is now recognised as a system involving flow of:

1. Information,

2. Marketing communications (promotion),

3. Materials,

4. Manpower,

5. Capital equipment and money.

It is no longer merely a collection of independent business establishments.

It is a system of flows:

1. Flow of goods and people,
2. Flow of ownership and risk of loss,
3. Flow of information,
4. Flow of promotion, ordering payment and financing,
5. Flow of negotiation and transaction.

Ownership, possession and promotion move forward. Ordering and payment move from consumers backward. Risk of loss, negotiating activity and information move forward as well as backward.

Distribution Channels – Choice of Distribution Channel

Channel of distribution is the route taken by the ownership right to the goods as the goods move from the primary producer to the ultimate consumer in the process of marketing.

Distribution channel represents a chain of middlemen (merchants and agents) participating in the distribution of goods, i.e., in the flow or movement of goods in the process of marketing. The route or channel includes both the manufacturer or primary producer and the ultimate consumer as well as all middlemen in distribution such as merchants, mercantile agents, banks, transport agencies, insurance companies, advertising agencies, warehousing companies and so on. All channel members are interrelated and form the total distribution system.

Marketing institutions in the machinery of distribution perform five important marketing functions:

1. Contacting or searching out of buyers and sellers,
2. Merchandising or matching goods to the market demands,
3. Creating demand or persuading and influencing the prospective buyers to favour a certain product and its sponsor (promotion),
4. Pricing the product or service in such a manner that it is acceptable to the buyers and it can ensure effective distribution, and
5. Physical distribution or transport and warehousing of goods at each stage in the process of distribution (physical distribution).

Please note that each of the aforesaid marketing function is expected to facilitate the process of exchange.

Sub-Divisions of Distribution System:

Distribution system has two subdivisions:

1. Channels of distribution.
2. Physical distribution.

The channel members such as mercantile agents, wholesalers and retailers are middlemen in distribution and they perform all marketing functions. Such middlemen are specialised in one or a few marketing functions.

These middlemen facilitate the process of exchange and create time, place and possession utilities through matching and sorting process. Sorting enables meeting or matching the supply with consumer demand.

Physical distribution looks after physical handling of goods, and assures maximum customer service. It aims at offering delivery of right goods at the right time and place to customers.

Physical distribution activities cover:

1. Order processing,

2. Handling of goods,

3. Packaging,

4. Warehousing,

5. Transportation,

6. Inventory control, and

7. Customer service.

All middlemen in distribution perform these functions, and they assure putting the product within an arms length of customer desire and demand.

Distribution Channels – Selection

The problem of selecting the most suitable channel of distribution for a product is complex. The most fundamental factor for channel choice and channel management is economic criteria, viz., cost and profit criteria. Profit organisations are primarily interested in cost minimisation in distribution and assurance of reasonable profit margin.

However, channel decisions are not made entirely on the basis of rational economic analysis. We have to consider a number of factors such as the nature of the product, market trends, competition outlook, pricing policies, typical consumer needs, as well as needs of the manufacturer himself.

The following are other critical factors:

1. Product:

(a) If a commodity is perishable or fragile, a producer prefers few and controlled levels of distribution. For perishable goods speedy movement needs shorter channel or route of distribution (b) For durable and standardised goods longer and diversified channel may be necessary, (c) For custom made product direct distribution to consumer or industrial user may be desirable,

(d) Systems approach needs package deal and shorter- channel serves the purpose, (e) For technical product requiring specialised selling and serving talents, we have the shortest channel (f) Products of high unit value are sold directly by travelling sales- force and not through middleman.

2. Market:

(a) For consumer market, retailer is essential, whereas in industrial market we can eliminate retailer, (b) If the market size is large, we have many channels, whereas in a small market direct selling may be profitable, (c) For highly concentrated markets, direct selling is enough but for widely scattered and diffused markets, we must have many channels, (d) Size and average frequency of customer's orders also influence the channel decision. In the sale of food products, we need both wholesaler and retailer.

Market means people with money and willing to purchase want-satisfying goods. Age, income group, sex, vocation, religion of customers will have to be studied to secure adequate information of market segments or target markets. Buying habits of customers and dealers will also influence our channel choice.

Consumer and dealer analysis will give us data on the number, type, location, buying habits of consumers and dealers. Channel choice needs this information. For example, desire for credit, preference for one- stop shopping, demand for personal services, amount of time and effort the customer is willing to spend—all are important factors in channel choice.

If ultimate buyers are numerous, the order is small, order frequency is great and buyers insist on the right to choose from a wide variety of brands/goods, we must have three or even more levels of distribution. Market considerations also govern mass distribution (through multiple channels) or selective/exclusive distribution through few or even one dealer. When service after sale is required, e.g., TV Sets, Refrigerators, etc., selective distribution is profitable.

3. Middlemen:

(a) Middlemen who can provide wanted marketing services will be given first preference. Of Course, they must be available. (b) The selected middlemen must offer maximum co-operation particularly in promotional services. They must accept marketing policies and programmes of the manufacturers and actively help them in their implementation, (c) The channel generating the largest sales volume at lower unit cost will be given top priority. This will minimise distribution cost.

4. Company:

(a) The company's size determines the size of the market, the size of its larger accounts and its ability to get middlemen's co-operation. A big firm may have shorter channel, (b) The company's product mix influences the pattern of channels. The broader the product line, the shorter will be the channel. If the product mix has greater depth or specialisation, the company can favour selective or exclusive dealerships,

(c) A company with substantial financial resources need not rely too much on the middlemen and can afford to reduce the levels of distribution. A weaker company has to depend on middlemen to secure financial and warehousing reliefs, (d) New companies rely heavily on middlemen due to lack of experience and ability of management. (e) A company desiring to exercise greater control over channel will prefer a shorter channel as it will facilitate better co-ordination communication and control.

(f) Heavy advertising and sales promotion can motivate middlemen to handle displays and join enthusiastically in the promotion campaign and co-operative publicity. In such cases even a longer chain of distribution can be profitable. Thus, quantity and quality of marketing services provided by the company can influence the channel choice directly.

5. Marketing Environment:
Marketing environment can also influence the channel decision. During recession or depression, shorter and cheaper channel is always preferable. In times of prosperity, we have a wider choice of channel alternatives. Technological inventions also have impact on distribution. The distribution of perishable goods even in distant markets become a reality due to cold storage facilities in transport and warehousing. Hence, this led to expanded role of intermediaries in the distribution of perishable goods.

6. Competitors:
Marketers closely watch the channels used by rivals. Many a time, similar channels may be desirable to bring about distribution of your products also. However, sometimes marketers deliberately avoid customary channels (dominated by rivals) and adopt different channel strategy. For instance, you may by-pass retail store channel (usually used by rivals) and adopt door- to-door sales (where there is no competition).

WHOLESALER
Meaning and Definition:
The word 'Wholesaler' has been derived from the word 'Wholesale' which means to sell goods in relatively large quantities or in bulk. A wholesaler, in the words of S.E. Thomas 'is a trader who purchases goods in large quantities from manufacturers and sells to retailers in small quantities.

The term 'wholesaler' applies only to a merchant middleman engaged in selling the goods in bulk quantities. Wholesaling includes all marketing transactions in which purchases are intended for resale or are used in marketing other products. Thus, we can say that a wholesaler is a person who buys goods from the producer in bulk quantities and forwards them in small quantities to retailers. So, a true wholesaler, as S.E. Thomas observes, "is himself neither a manufacturer nor a retailer, but acts as a link between the two". He is a vital link in the channel of distribution.

Introduction

The American Marketing Association has defined the wholesaler as "a business unit which buys and resells the merchandise to the retailers and the merchants or to the industrial, institutional and commercial users but does not sell insignificant amounts to the ultimate consumers."

"The wholesaler is one who buys goods on a large scale with the objective of selling them at a profit in smaller quantities. He buys from the producers that is the extractor or manufacturerand sells to the retailers, and is, therefore, the connecting link between these two"

Wholesalers occupy a pivotal place in the marketing channel set-up. In most cases they perform several critical functions invaluable to the smooth flow of goods, ownership, finance, and information. Several channel systems however, do not involve a wholesaler or distributor and directly connect the manufacturing unit to the retailers who are in contact with the customers. Or else, the system connects directly to the customers.

However, in these instances, either the manufacturer or the retailer (or in certain instances the customer) performs all the activities that a wholesaler will perform. Of course, the nature of the product distributed, and the consumption pattern determine the need for a wholesaler in channel systems.

For instance, high-value items such as cars or laptops can be directly sold to customers without the need for a level between the manufacturer and the retailer. Wholesalers are also known by several different terms such as distributors, dealers, and resellers.

Most of these players perform certain important functions that are essential to the overall consumption experience of the channel. Wholesalers could also vertically integrate downwards and operate retail outlets, in which case they become very powerful.

In fast moving consumer goods (FMCG), wholesalers are often much more powerful than the retailers, as they are much more bigger and the manufacturer relies more on the wholesalers for several critical functions such as finance and ownership, rather than on retailers.

Wholesalers are also often part of the channel information system and are therefore more crucial to the overall information flow in the channel system compared to retailers. Wholesalers can either be multi-brand wholesalers, where they offer their services to several manufacturer (even competing manufacturers), or exclusive wholesalers where they are tied in with just one manufacturer. For a manufacturer, one of the biggest channel decisions is to decide whether to rely on an exclusive wholesaler or a multi-brand wholesaler. There are cost and control implications tied to this decision.

In several cases, wholesalers are quite big in terms of the volume of business they handle, to become extremely powerful in the channel set-up. There are several ways of appointing and controlling wholesalers.

One manner, which is gaining popularity recurrently, is through a legally binding contract signed by the wholesaler and the manufacturer. Such an arrangement is called a franchisee arrangement. A franchisee arrangement has several advantages over conventional transaction-based arrangements.

Characteristic of Wholesaler

The main **characteristics of wholesaler** are:

1. He buys and sells goods in large quantities.
2. He deals only with a few types of products.
3. He acts as a middleman between the producers and retailers.
4. He usually makes cash purchases and sells goods on credit to the retailers.
5. He does not sell goods to consumers.
6. He operates in a particular area determined by producers

Importance of wholesalers

The importance of wholesaler in our marketing system can better be understood by investigating as to how they serve the

1. Manufacturers
2. Retailers
3. Society

Manufacturers

The services which are provided by the wholesaler to the producers are as under:-

- Concentration on production
- Facilities large scale production
- Information about consumer behaviors
- Regulation of production
- Reliving producers from keeping stock
- Financial assistance

Retailers

The services which are provided by the wholesaler to the retailers are as under:-

- Relief from keeping a huge stock
- Financial help
- Not affected by price fluctuations
- Provision of information
- Transportation facilities
- Trade discount
- Benefit of specialization

Society

The services which are provided by the wholesaler to the society are as under:-

- Availability of goods to the consumers
- Stability in price
- Low in price

Knowledge about new products
Types of Wholesalers:
The wholesalers may be classified under the following headings:
(A) On the basis of area covered:
(a) Local wholesalers, who distribute the goods from the producer to the consumer of a particular locality or area.
(b) State wholesalers, who function in a particular state or province.

(c) Country-wide wholesales who are located at the main business centres of the country and who distribute goods throughout the length and breadth of the country.

(B) On the basis of the goods they deal in:

It is the most used grouping of wholesale concerns. According to T.N. Backman, 'it is not easy to define their limits of operations on any particular basis or criterion, but usually three bases are selected:

(a) Methods of distributing goods: (b) sources of supply; and (c) the use of the goods by the consumers.'

(C) On the basis of methods of operation:

(a) Full-function wholesales-who perform the entire range of wholesale functions, viz., assembling, storage, transportation, packing, financing and risk-bearing.

(b) Limited function wholesalers-who perform only limited or specific functions out of the full range of wholesale functions. They include:

(i) Rack Jobbers-wholesalers who sell special products viz., household wares and cosmetic/toiletries to retailers.

(ii) Truck wholesalers-who combine selling, delivery, and collection in one operation. They carry only specific type of products, usually perishable and semi-perishable goods.

(iii) Cash-and-carry wholesalers-who sell their stocks to retailers on 'cash and carry' basis. The retailers come to the wholesalers' godown, select their requirements and pay cash on the spot and take away the goods.

(iv) Drop shipment wholesalers-who do not actually handle the goods in which they deal in but leave the storage and transportation functions for the producers whom they represent to perform. Here, the producer directly dispatches the goods to the retailers, but the bill is forwarded through the wholesaler, who, in turn, claims it from the retailers. Such wholesalers deal in goods which bear high cost of transportation.

(c) Merchant wholesalers.

They are of the following types:

(i) Wholesalers proper:

They are those merchants who deal only in the buying and selling activities and do not engage in manufacturing activities. They buy goods in bulk from the manufacturers and sell them in bulk to retailers. They also maintain their own warehouses for storing the goods.

(ii) Manufacturer wholesalers:

They combine the twin functions of manufacturing and selling and operate as both manufacturers and wholesalers. They usually purchase goods in their crude form, and after processing in their plant, sell them in a refined form to retailers. Their production operations are relatively simple and their main activity is that of selling.

(iii) Mill-supply wholesalers/Industrial Distributors:

Such wholesalers sell a wide range of goods to industrial units, who, in turn, use them for their manufacturing operations. These wholesalers buy goods in bulk quantities from producers/growers and sell them to industrial mills. For example, a wholesaler may purchase raw tobacco from growers and sell them to factories which manufacture cigarettes.

(D) On the basis of their line of product:

(a) General merchandise wholesalers:

Wholesalers who deal in a number of items of general merchandise, ranging from food products to household appliances.

(b) General line wholesalers:

Who offer complete stock in one major line, e.g., stationery goods or may be hardware appliances, etc.

(c) Specialised wholesalers:

Who deal only in specialised goods such as food products c: electrical goods, etc. They help those retailers who wish to buy a wide range of goods of the same line.

Functions of a Wholesaler:

A wholesaler performs the following functions:

(i) Assembling:

A wholesaler buys goods from producers who are scattered far and wide and assembles them in his warehouse for the purpose of the retailers.

(ii) Storage:

After arranging and assembling the products from producers, wholesaler stores them in his warehouse and releases them in proper and required quantities as and when they are required by retailers. Since there is always a time-lag between production and consumption, therefore, the manufactured goods are to be stored carefully till they are demanded by retailers. Thus, a wholesaler performs the storage function in order to save the goods from deterioration and also to make these goods available when they are demanded.

(iii) Transportation:

Wholesalers buy goods in bulk from the producers and transport them to their own godowns. Also, they provide transportation facility to retailers' by transporting the goods from their warehouses to the retailers' shops. Some wholesalers purchase in bulk, therefore, they can avail the economies of freight on bulk purchases.

(iv) Financing:

A wholesaler provides credit facility to retailers who are in need of financial assistance.

(v) Risk-bearing:

A wholesaler bears all the trade risks arising out of the sudden fall in prices of goods or by way of damage/spoilage or destruction of goods in his warehouse. The risk of bad debt as a result of nonpayment by retailers who have purchased on credit, also falls on the wholesalers. Thus a wholesaler bears all the trade and financial risks of the business.

(vi) Grading and Packing:

A wholesaler sorts out the goods according to their quality and then packs them in appropriate containers. Thus, he performs the marketing function of grading and packing also.

(vii) Providing Marketing Information:

Wholesalers provide valuable market information to retailers and manufacturers. The retailers are informed about the quality and type of goods available in the market for sale, whereas the manufacturers are informed about the changes in tastes and fashions of consumers so that they may produce the goods of the desired level of taste and fashion.

(viii) Facilitating Disbursement and Sale:

Wholesalers sell their goods to retailers who are scattered far and wide. Retailers approach them when their stocks are exhausted from further replenishment. Thus, wholesalers help in the dispersion process of marketing.

Retailer

A retaileris a person or business that you purchase goods from. Retailers typically don't manufacture their own items. They purchase goods from a manufacturer or a wholesaler and sell these goods to consumers in small quantities.

Characteristics of a Retailer

- In the entire distribution chain, a retailer is considered to be the final link, who deals directly with the customer.

- A retailer purchases in bulk from the wholesalers and sells the products to the customers in small quantities.
- A retailer essentially maintains a variety of merchandise.
- The aim of a retailer is to achieve maximum satisfaction by exceeding their expectations and delivering exceptional services.

Functions of Retailers

(i) Merchandising:

Merchandising covers the activities of planning and supervising the marketing of goods at the right places, times and prices and in right quantities to the right customers. It facilitates a proper coordination of supply with demand. The marketing activities of assembling (buying) of goods from different producers and wholesalers and preparing them for resale to consumers at a profit are called merchandising activities.

Retailers have to assemble and maintain enough stocks of a variety of goods so that they can meet adequately consumer demand and fulfil consumer expectations.

(ii) Warehousing:

In order to meet consumer demand promptly, the retailer must keep goods in ready stock and avoid an out-of-stock position as far as possible. Hence, he should have reasonable storage facilities.

(iii) Selling:

Successful buying must be combined with efficient methods of selling, advertising and sales promotion. The retailer is the last point of sale in the machinery of distribution. Retail trade is an important branch of commerce where goods are directly sold to the final consumer.

(iv) Risk-Bearing:

Goods are bought and stored in .anticipation of sales at a profit. Consumer demand is always changing. Prices, too, fluctuate. Hence, the risk of loss due to changes in demand and changes in prices is always present. Then, again, there is always the possibility of the loss of goods by fire, theft, riot, deterioration in quality, etc., the risk of loss due to changes in -demand, changes in style and fashions, changes in prices are borne by retailers.

(v) Grading and Packing:

A retailer may have to perform the marketing functions of branding, grading and packaging when lie deals with ungraded goods received from producers.

(vi) Grant of Credit:

Credit sales offer a lot of convenience to salaried and wage-earning people. A credit sale is a sales promotion device, for it encourages permanent and regular customers to deal with one retailer. People who "run an account" with the retailer go to one shop. For the sale of durable and costly goods to consumers, a hire-purchase or an installment sale facility is offered. In its absence, the sale of costly consumer durable goods may not be possible on a large scale. Many people buy goods on hire-purchase or HP.

(vii) Guide to Wholesaler or Producer:

Manufacturers and wholesalers can secure first-hand information of the wants of consumers from retailers, because retailers have personal contacts with their consumers. They can guide manufacturers to produce those articles which are likely to be in great demand in the near future due to changes in the tastes and habits of consumers.

The retailer is the best source for the determination of the pulse of demand, e.g., changing consumer preferences and tastes, and changes in fashions. Marketing plans are based on probable consumer demand.

(viii) Last Outlet in the Chain of Distribution:

In relation to producers and wholesalers, retailers act as the last outlet for the distribution of goods within the country. A retailer is the connecting link between the wholesaler and the consumers. Individual sales in small quantities are the responsibility of the retailer. In the absence of retailers, it would be impossible to distribute goods to ultimate consumers, and most of our wants will remain unsatisfied. In short, the entire trade will be paralyzed.

(ix) Advertising, Salesmanship and Sales Promotion:

Manufactured goods are worthless unless they pass the acid test of retail distribution. The retailer must employ efficient methods of promotion, i.e., salesmanship, advertising and sales promotion. Nothing can be sold without the means of promotion or means of marketing communication.

Middleman

In a distribution or transaction chain, a middleman acts as an intermediary, facilitating communication between the parties involved. Middlemen are experts at completing critical functions in the purchase and selling of goods as they move from manufacturers to final buyers. They usually don't make anything, but they do have a lot of market expertise, therefore they charge a fee or a commission for their services.

Types of Middleman

There are two types of middlemen: merchants and agents.

1. **Merchants:**
holesalers and merchants, for example, buy and resell their products. They take ownership of inventories and are responsible for the costs of storage and distribution. They gain money by selling the things for more than they paid for them. The distinction is referred to as "markup." A shopkeeper to a major multinational firm with international activities is all examples of merchant middlemen. Larger middlemen may specialise on a specific market area or main skill, such as delivery, advertising, or storage.

2. **Agents**
Brokers and real estate agents, for example, specialise in transactional agreements. They don't accept responsibility for what they're selling. They make money instead by charging fees. a charge or commission for facilitating a transaction.
Brokers, for example, operate as go-betweens for investors and the stock exchange. They charge a brokerage fee in exchange for providing trading services, investment advice, and solutions to its clients.

Function of middleman
In a marketplace, middlemen fulfil the following tasks:

1. They provide producers with vital information and feedback about consumer behaviour, changing tastes and styles, upcoming competitors, and so on.
2. They allow manufacturers to focus on their primary role of manufacturing by managing supplementary functions such as storage, distribution, advertising, and insurance. On behalf of the producers, they advertise the items to the consumers.
3. Manufacturers receive financial services from middlemen such as banks and other financial organisations.
4. They ensure that consumers have access to goods and services at the appropriate time, in the right amount, and in the right location.
5. For fear of losing money, buyers and sellers are typically hesitant to take on market risk. The risks of the process chain are assumed by the middlemen.

Elimination of middleman

The term "**middleman**" describes an intermediary between a producer and an end customer. In a typical distribution channel, the **middleman** is the wholesaler or the retailer. Manufacturers would **eliminate** the **middleman** by selling products directly to retail stores or consumers.In theory, eliminating the middlemen sounds like a good idea. This would help to lower costs for consumers who could buy products for less and for businesses who could sell their products for less. However, this may not be the most practical idea.

Middlemen provide an important service. Think about the groceries you buy. The grocery store is an example of a middleman in business. When you buy groceries, you can get various products all in one place. You don't have to go directly to the farmer to buy milk, meat, and vegetables. You don't have to go directly to a bakery to buy bread and other bakery products. The same can be said for all of the products in the grocery store. While middlemen add cost to a product, when thinking of the time and expense you would have to incur to buy all of your items directly from the supplier, you will very likely be better off by purchasing most of your products from a middleman than by purchasing them directly from the producer.

Important Questions:

1. Define selection of distribution channel
2. Write short notes on level of channels
3. Explain the important of function of distribution channel
4. What is the factors affecting choice of channel distribution
5. Give short notes on competitive factor, market related factor and environment factor.
6. Write short on distribution channel system.
7. Explain the selection of distribution channel
8. Who is wholesaler
9. Define wholesaler
10. List down the important of wholesaler
11. Write the types of wholesaler
12. What is the Characteristic of wholesaler
13. Define Retailers

14. Explain the function of retailers
15. Write down the characteristic of retailers
16. Explain the functions of retailers
17. Who is the middleman
18. Explain the elimination of middleman
19. Write down the types of middleman
20. Explain the function of middleman

IV
Pricing

Product Marketing

Product marketing is the practice of promoting and selling a product to a customer in a strategic way. Product marketing also serves as a link between product development and increased market awareness. Product-oriented marketing works with a variety of departments, including product, marketing, sales, and customer service, to improve the product and guarantee it fits the needs of the target market. A new product that is available to the broader public the product market is defined by a single statement: product type, customer needs (functional needs), customer type, and geographic location. When it comes to pitching, a product market is something that is mentioned. Product marketing is a strategic marketing function that connects product development and marketing communications. A product marketing manager's principal responsibility is to establish and size target markets and value propositions. Positioning and sales enablement are two other critical tasks. Product management is concerned with the fundamentals of product creation within a company, whereas product marketing is concerned with selling the product to prospects, customers, and other interested parties. Product marketing differs from other marketing jobs such as social media marketing, marketing communications ("marcom"), online marketing, advertising, marketing strategy, and public relations as a job function within a company, though product marketers may use outbound marketing channels such as the internet for their product.

7 P's of product marketing

Product marketers frequently use the 7 P's as a set of guiding principles for developing product marketing strategies. Let's take a look at each of the seven P's one by one.

1. **Product**: Customers' pain areas must be understood by product marketers, who must then collaborate closely with product managers to design a product that can address these issues. In other words, the product should meet the expectations of the buyers.
2. **Price**: Product marketers must consider the broader marketplace, the intensity of demand, and other rivals when determining the ideal price for a certain product. The pricing of the product should be examined and reexamined by the product marketing team to ensure that it always offers good value for money.
3. **Place**: In this situation, place refers to the location where your target customers can locate your product. Nowadays, the term "place" in product marketing can refer to both a physical location such as a store or a market corner, as well as an online business. A software company, for example, will almost certainly sell its products through an internet distribution channel.
4. **Promotion**: Promotion does not only refer to advertising in the context of product marketing. Brand recognition, product differentiation, demand generation, and lead generation are all part of it. Overall, product message is what advertising entails.
5. **Process:** In product marketing, the process relates to how a customer purchases and receives their chosen product. To reduce the number of abandoned carts, an online business owner, for example, must consider how to simplify and improve their checkout page. Meanwhile, a physical store owner must pay close attention to how their products are displayed on the shelf.
6. **People:** People are those within or outside your business who perform all of the work necessary to bring a product to market and ensure its long-term viability. As a product marketer, you must be able to coordinate these individuals in order to reach the desired outcome.
7. **There is physical proof:** When it comes to marketing a product, gathering and analysing feedback is crucial. Is the feedback indicating that your product is satisfactory? No one wants to release a product that isn't up to par.

Objectives of Product Marketing

The following Objectives are frequently engaged in product marketing:

- Product marketing is involved in the positioning, messaging, consumer base development, and overall market strategy for releasing a product before it is launched.
- Following the launch of a product, product marketing focuses on increasing sales by increasing demand, adoption, and overall success of the product. Long after a product launch, the product marketing process continues to ensure that the right people are aware of the product, that they understand how to use it, and that their requirements and feedback are integrated into the product life cycle.

Next, we'll look at how product managers use a marketing funnel to better understand and capitalise on their customers' buying habits.

Function of Product Marketing

1. **Consumer exploration**

   Product marketing is critical in defining the optimum target market and researching potential buyers prior to a product launch. Product marketing teams do several interviews and market surveys to learn about customers' biggest challenges, behaviours, likes and dislikes, and so on. Key insights assist the product development team in tailoring product features to answer the difficulties that target consumers are experiencing. Following the product's debut, product marketers collaborate closely with the sales and customer care teams to collect consumer feedback and make practical recommendations to the development team.

2. **Rival exploration**

   Product marketing conducts research to understand rivals and alternatives before developing competitive advantages in order to bring a new product to market. What are the features that are a must-have? What are the distinguishing characteristics? What are the most important functions? What are the differentiating functions? After all, it is product marketers that are in charge of the inquiries.

3. **Storytelling about solutions**

   Product marketing shares success stories about how the product provides actual benefits to customers and how they use it to achieve their objectives. The problem statement is presented by the product manager. The product marketer, on the other hand, is the one who creates solution stories. From the standpoint of product marketing, it must be about selling an experience as well as a product. No one wants a product, in reality. People are looking for a solution to their issues. Only describing features, advantages, and data means you're missing out on a lot of opportunity to engage customers. However, if you deliver a memorable and emotive story, you will win the game.

4. **Positioning of the product**

Product marketers develop an internal document to inform everyone in the organisation on the product's market position. The strategic practice of positioning is used while creating a new product or improving an existing one.

5. **Messages about products**

The product description that is communicated with the rest of the world is known as product messaging. The target audiences will be able to grasp the product's benefits and how it operates as a result of this. Other marketing operations, including as advertising, content authoring, and social media posting, are shaped by product messaging. It's crucial to keep product communications consistent across all media.

6. **Product dissemination is being pushed**

Product marketers may ensure that their product reaches their target clients by having a thorough understanding of the product and target audiences. Product marketing teams design and implement strategies for interacting with customers through various communication channels. Product marketing tests and analyses distribution channels on a regular basis in order to improve their performance.

7. **Workforce development**

The product marketing team explains the product's value and differentiating benefits if the product management team demonstrates it. Product marketing accelerates internal training across the organisation so that all teams can provide a consistent customer experience. Internal communication is clearly just as vital as exterior communication. Product marketers are in charge of getting everyone and everything ready for the launch of a new product. For instance, the website is ready to launch, and the customer service team is ready to respond to client inquiries. To summarize, product marketing has numerous advantages for a company. It locates the appropriate goods and delivers it to the appropriate client. Product marketing boosts income and profits while also ensuring the company's long-term viability for small companies. One or a few products can be the entire firm in small businesses or start-ups. The marketing of a product is basically the marketing of the company as a whole. It is the only method to expand your company.

Product marketing provides crucial data to add new features to a current product or determine which new products should be produced as your company grows. The business owner can recognise market wants and develop successful plans using these insights.In today's dynamic and increasingly competitive market, product marketing is a critical component of any company's success.

Service Marketing

Promoting of items and administrations includes various methodologies because of the dissimilarities in their attributes. While in item showcasing, the point is to satisfy the necessities and needs of the objective populace. As against, in assistance showcasing, the firm looks to make a decent connection with the client, to win their trust.

Item advertising is the way toward putting up an item for sale to the public. This incorporates choosing the item's situating and informing, dispatching the item, and guaranteeing sales reps and clients get it. Item promoting means to drive the interest and use of the item. Item promoting doesn't stop once the item has gone to showcase (in the event that it did, indeed, item advertisers at a one-item organization wouldn't have a lot to do after the item's dispatch). The way toward showcasing an item endures well after its dispatch to guarantee the ideal individuals know about the item, those individuals realize how to utilize it, and that the requirements and input of those individuals are being tuned in to over the item's lifecycle.

The two most significant exercises attempted by the business is creation or acquisition of items and its dispersion to the end client. The acquisition of crude materials and its change into a completed item is a simple work. Nonetheless, the payment of the item is a demanding one, on the grounds that making a spot for an item in the market is somewhat troublesome errand, as the market is now overwhelmed with lacs and lacs of items, where nobody thinks about your item and in this manner the showcasing comes into the image.

These days, advertising isn't kept to the item; however benefits, thoughts, property, encounters and even individuals are showcased. The advertising exercises are pointed toward making an impression of the item or administration in the buyer mind, in such a way, that your image turns into an equivalent for that specific item or administration.

Objectives of Service Marketing:

Any organization's services have missions and objectives that must be met in order for the service to be effective.

The following are the goals of service marketing in any organisation:

i. Define the service's goals, policies, and procedures, as well as the best means to put them into action.

ii. Determine service plans, techniques, and strategies for efficient service performance; (iii) Determine service quality and design for service performance; and

iii. Determine the directions and fundamental criteria for managing customers' care services.

iv. Determine service goals and market categories based on client profiles,

v. Determine the most comfortable, convenient, and straightforward service delivery procedure; any organization's services have missions and objectives that must be met in order for the service to be effective.

vi. Provide service staff with the necessary training, salary, advancement, and growth opportunities.

vii. To ensure that service expectations and service delivery are in sync,

viii. To make effective operational service quality of performance judgments.

ix. To oversee service operations in which value is realised for the services provided,

x. To establish effective and goal-oriented customer relationships,

xi. To monitor and apply service performance quality parameters,

xii. Overcome and resolve issues and obstacles originating from service delivery.

Importance of Service Marketing:

1. **Secondary and primary school development** - Different services are required for the smooth operation of the primary and secondary sectors. As a result, the service industry as a whole plays a critical role in the smooth operation of various sectors.

2. **Increased employment** - The service industry employs people in a variety of industries, including aviation, brokerages, tourism, hospitality, software, entertainment, retail, and BPOs. As a result, the entire country benefits.

3. **An increase in national income**- The expansion and growth of the service industry will help to boost national income. The country would have the same level of development and progress as any other sector.

4. **Support for fundamental services** - The service sector helps the country's basic services such as post offices, insurance, courts, transportation, banking, telecommunications, educational institutes, and hospitality. These services are essential in the daily lives of ordinary people.

5. **Improve a country's image** - Services such as ITES and BPO will improve a country's international image. In the eyes of the world, this indicates a bright future for the country.

6. **Increase in exports** - More demand will come from countries beyond international borders for high-quality service sectors. These, in turn, increase exports and improve a country's economic stability by bringing in foreign currency.

7. **More opportunities for women** - Working women are in more demand in the service sector. This has provided unprecedented opportunities for women to work and compete on an equal footing with males.

Characteristics of Services Marketing:

1. **Perishability:** Perishability is one of the most important characteristics of services marketing. Once used, the advantages received from services cannot be resold, preserved, stored, or returned. It is not possible to return or transfer a service once it has been delivered. A disappointed consumer, for example, cannot ask a barber to reverse the haircut he has gotten.

2. **The inseparability:** The service provider creates the service and the customer consumes it at the same time. A cobbler polishes his customer's shoes as part of his service, and the customer's problem is fixed on the spot.

3. **The act of providing service is a performance:** Services are provided in addition to the production of goods. In the vast majority of circumstances, services are unrelated to any physical product.

4. **There is no transfer of ownership with services:** Typically, a service does not result in the acquisition of any property. In other words, unlike product marketing, there is no transfer of title or ownership. Another result of concurrent production and consumption is that service providers find themselves acting as both a component of the product and an integral component of the consumer's service experience. You become the owner of a product when you buy it, whether it's a pencil, book, shirt, refrigerator, or car. You may pay for the use of a product or service, but you never own it. In the event of a service, the payment is not for the purchase of products or facilities, but rather for their use, access, or hire.

Functions of Service Marketing:

Different services are handled and controlled by an individual or a group of people in the context of business phenomena. In addition, private owners or government entities are linked to the services. These services either directly or indirectly promote business or serve as a complement to it.

The following are some examples of service functions:

1. **Business Services**: The symbolic role of services has evolved in order to boost the size and composition of various business operations. When a businessman tries to make money by providing services, the services may be considered a part of the firm. For the sake of business, businessmen coordinate profit motives and service motives. In this context, services play an important role in coordinating and developing business activities such as trade and commerce in order to increase value ads, improve quality, enhance retailing activities, and expand market shares. Appropriate services may be able to raise the level of strength and opportunities and overcome the adverse condition of a company phenomenon.

2. **Personal Services:** Marketers may be able to establish personal services ideology based on the concept of salesmanship. Personal services foster two-way communication between service providers and their clients. It is based on various characteristics such as intelligence, good looks, initiative, integrity, ethical behavior, honesty, cooperativeness, social rationality, and adherence to code of conducts. There are a variety of personal services available, including health care, electricians, plumbers, restaurants, technical assistance, beauty salons, and driving services,

among others. In the current state of the service sector, personal services play a significant and pivotal role.

3. **Professional Services:** In service sector, the professional services have been most important and decisional role. These services are based on specified knowledge, education, training and experience. It aims to achieve the profit as well as service motives of any organization. The role, contribution and attitudes of professional persons are required to follow several norms and provisions as laid down in the code of conducts of professionals. These services may develop new avenues i.e. mannerism, behaviour, styles, values, intelligences and integrity by means of research, investigations and experiences. In service sector, the main professional services may be health care, counseling, tutoring, medical, technical, tax consultation, accounting, legal, computer services and maintenance etc.

4. **Distribution Services:** In current marketing systems, businesspeople and entrepreneurs provide a variety of services through distribution channels. Within it, they provide a variety of services such as standardisation, product delivery, risk bearing, packing, warehousing, transportation, business possibilities, credit sales, promotional services, and grievance handling, among others. These services are helping to speed up the merchandising environment in the workplace.

5. **Consultants:** When a person or a group of people provide counseling or consulting services, they are referred to as consultants. They may be required to work with certain businesses at times. These services should be viewed as decision-making aspects such as policy formulations, missions and objectives, situational analyses, behavioural perspectives, and environmental considerations, among others. Management, organisational, project development, market strategies, tax planning, and investment planning, as well as medical and health care, and domestic concerns, are examples of these services. Counseling services are provided by experts in the majority of cases.

6. **Communication Services:** Communication is an important and dynamic component of any business. In any organisation, there are different types of communication, such as communication based on direction, scope, organisation state, and media, among others. Furthermore, there are other modes of communication, such as oral, written, and verbal. Visual symbols, body language, tele-communication, electronic media, and online services are all examples of nonverbal

communication systems that advertise services. These services are required to meet particular objectives, such as environmental awareness, increased reliability, promotional tasks, expertizing services, and motivational features in the context of services. Mobile phones, telephones, fax machines, radios, postal services, and televisions are among the most common modes of communication.

7. **Financial Services:** The most essential mechanism for economic transformation is probably financial services. Its primary goal is to devise and refine methods for coordinating savings and investment, as well as to boost capital production in our economy. Money loans, term deposits, credit facilities, tax advice, resource mobilisation, charity, donations, auditing, and a variety of investments are only a few of the financial services available. These services are provided by a single person or a group of people.

8. **Banking and Insurance Services:** Banking and insurance services have contributed to a variety of societal developments. Their main responsibilities include coordinating savings and investments, providing various banking and insurance services, developing capital production methods, and developing resource mobilisation methods and to improve economic security, among other things. These services also provide a parallel platform for generating and developing economic resources at various levels and compositions.

9. **Advertising Services:** In today's corporate world, several individuals and groups have been hired to provide advertising services. Advertising media's effectiveness as a driver of corporate performance has been demonstrated. The underlying principle of societal values, creativity, rationality, responsiveness, and truthfulness can be used by advertising services to establish and improve company attitudes and behaviour. These services are extremely valuable and decisive in increasing the effectiveness of advertising initiatives.

10. **Public Services:** Public services arose from the welfare state concept and are linked to the protection of human rights. Their goals are to produce and promote real and fair service performance in society, as well as commitment, integrity, loyalty, and a sense of humour. The principal public services are managed and controlled by civil administration at the municipal level. Civil administration, municipal services, public works, public health, and engineering services such as water and power supply transportation, public administration, and security are among the most

important services. These services provide the way for a long-term transition to the welfare state idea.

11. **Medical Services:** Medical services are governed and controlled by either the government or the private sector. Inevitably, these services are more involved with civil law and administration. In terms of people and diseases, the medical services have focused on four primary sectors. Consultations, adequate investigation, treatment, and medicines and treatments are the categories covered. Medical services must provide fair and reasonable behaviour, prompt services, human values, the majority of mannerism attitudes, and non-exploitation attitudes to the people of our society.

12. **Tourism services:** Tourism services are widely regarded as the most broad, largest, and fastest-growing industry in the world. Tourism is a major driver of economic development. Tourism services include ethnical, historical, religious, cultural, adventure, and recreation, among others. Various tourism services, such as health care, boats, recreations, bars, restaurants, cultural events, and water parks, are provided in tourist destinations. We should use ethical standards and behaviours to protect and use these services.

13. **Transportation Services:** Transportation is the sum total of all mechanical means and organisations that aid people and things in moving from one location to another. It falls under the heading of business services. There are several major modes of transportation available, including road, land, air, and water.

14. **Entertainment Services:** Entertainment services have evolved as a result of new and evolving trends in standard of living, as well as the expanding role of young in society. Every individual is obliged to obtain an increasing number of entertainment services at their highest degree. The key services available at the moment are video, cinema, theatre, WhatsApp dramas, and circus.

15. **Postal services:** Postal services are one of our society's oldest and most acceptable services. Correspondence, savings, investment, and money transfer are examples of key postal services. The postal service has a vast network for promoting various services such as communication, commodities shipping, and savings and investment. The expansion and development of postal services aids the growth of businesses.

16. **Legal Services:** Legal services are a crucial and decision-making service in society. They provide various rules and regulations to our society's

creation and establishment of fair and equitable behaviour and responses. They also provide many provisions and directions in order to create an ideal citizen and defend our constitution's dignity.

Definition of Product Marketing

The entire process, right from the market analysis, to delivering product to the customer and receiving feedback, is called product marketing. The process is aimed at finding out the right market for its product and its placement in such a way that it gets good customer response. It entails promotion and sale of a product to its target audience, i.e. prospective and existing buyers.

Various activities involved in the product marketing involves analysis of the market, identification of consumer demand, designing and development of product, pricing, pitching of a new product, communicating, advertising, positioning, distributing, selling, review and feedback.

Example: Marketing for tangible objects like books, handbags, laptops, mobiles, clothes and so on.

Definition of Service Marketing

When a person or business entity promotes services it offers to its customers or clients, it is known as service marketing. It is aimed at providing solutions to the problems or difficulties of the clients. It includes both business-to-business (B2B) and business-to-consumer (B2C) marketing.

A service is an act of performing something for someone in exchange for adequate consideration. It is intangible, consumed at the time of its production, can't be inventoried and resold. Each service offering is unique in itself because it cannot be repeated exactly alike, even if the service is rendered by the same person.

Example: Marketing of professional services, beauty parlours or salon, spa, coaching centres, health services, telecommunication, etc.

In the focuses given underneath, the contrasts between item showcasing and administration advertising is explained:

Key Differences Between Product Marketing and Service Marketing

- The interaction in which the advertising exercises are adjusted to advance and sell a particular item for a specific portion is called item showcasing. The advertising of financial exercises, offered by the business to its customers for sufficient thought, is known as administration showcasing.

- In an item advertising, just 4 P's of the showcasing blend are relevant which are item, value, spot and advancement, however on account of administration promoting, three more P's are added to the ordinary advertising blend, which are individuals, measure and actual presence.
- When an item is showcased, the organization offers esteem, as it satisfies client's prerequisites. Alternately, when administration is promoted by an organization, it offers a relationship to its customers.
- One thing to be noticed that, in item showcasing, the organization advances something whose possession can be moved/exchanged to another gathering. Be that as it may, on account of administration advertising, the organization advances something, whose proprietorship can nor be moved nor it is exchanged to the next gathering.
- item promoting, items arrive at the purchasers, as they can be shipped starting with one spot then onto the next through different conveyance channels. Dissimilar to support showcasing, where clients go to the administrations or the specialist co-op visit client since administrations can't be moved, they are area based.
- Products are unmistakable in nature, they can be felt and contacted, which make its advancement simpler. Then again, administrations are elusive, individuals can just experience it, thus showcasing of administrations is somewhat troublesome.
- If the nature of a specific item isn't sufficient, or it doesn't satisfy the ideal prerequisite, it tends to be gotten back to the dealer. In any case, it is outlandish on account of administrations, in light of the fact that once the administrations are conveyed, they can't be reclaimed. Thus, the promoting of administrations, ought to be finished remembering the returnability factor.
- In item showcasing, the item can be isolated from its maker, thus they are strong and can be stocked. Despite what might be expected, in assistance showcasing, administrations can not be isolated from its source, for example specialist organization. Consequently the creation and utilization of administrations are concurrent; they are short-lived.
- Product offered by an organization under a specific portion are normalized; they can't be changed or adjusted according to client's necessity. Interestingly, administrations offered by an organization are exceptionally factor and can be handily modified according to the necessities.

- It is a human propensity, that we react rapidly, to what we see and it is a significant expert, of item advertising that it catches our eye, and energizes deals. As against this, administrations can't be seen it must be capable thus the reaction it somewhat sluggish, while advertising administrations.
- In item promoting, the nature of the item can be estimated by making a correlation between different items, yet this is only inverse in assistance advertising, where the estimation of administrations is unimaginable.

Regardless of whether, its item advertising or a help showcasing, the undertaking is similarly difficult. In any case, with the previous, there are a few favorable circumstances like substantial quality, detachability, toughness, adaptability, and so on which the last needs, making it somewhat troublesome. Exhibit of item or administration is probably the most ideal approaches to advance it. Further, informal exchange additionally helps in promoting them.

Meaning of price

Cost is the sum we pay for merchandise, administrations or thoughts. The term cost is known by an assortment of names in various areas of the economy. For instance, cost is known as admission in the vehicle area; expense in training; lease in land and in specific administrations it is known as charge. As a rule, the cost is the trade an incentive between the vender and purchaser. Along these lines, cost is the cash charged by an advertiser for his item or administration. For the advertiser, value covers the complete market offering. A definitive client considers cost as a penance of his buying power. For the purchaser, it represents quality and amount of the help purchased. Cost is the wellspring of income and a superb determinant of benefit for the specialist co-op. In the assistance area. cost mirrors the idea of connection among client and supplier.

What is pricing

Valuing is comparable to the absolute help offering. Estimating incorporates the brand name, conveyance and different advantages. Valuing makes an interpretation of the subjective contribution into quantitative terms.

Objectives of Pricing:

- **Survival** - The target of valuing for any organization is to fix a value that is sensible for the customers and furthermore for the maker to get by on the lookout. Each organization is at risk for getting precluded from the market due to thorough rivalry, change in client's inclinations and taste. Thusly, while deciding the expense of an item all the factors and fixed expense ought to be contemplated. When the endurance stage is over the organization can take a stab at additional benefits.

- **Expansion of current benefits** - The majority of the organization attempts to grow their overall revenue by assessing the interest and supply of administrations and merchandise on the lookout. So the pricing is fixed by the item's interest and the substitute for that item. In the event that the interest is high, the cost will likewise be high.
- **Ruling the market**-Company's force low figure for the merchandise and enterprises to get hold of enormous market size. The strategy assists with expanding the deal by expanding the interest and prompting low creation cost.
- **A market for a creative idea** - Here, the organization charge an excessive cost for their item and administrations that are exceptionally imaginative and utilize bleeding edge innovation. The cost is high a direct result of high creation cost. Cell phone, electronic contraptions are a couple of models.

Pricing of services

Pricing is an important aspect of marketing. One of the most important aspects of the marketing mix is price. It is the only and most significant component of a company's marketing mix that generates money. Pricing should be done in a smart manner by businesses. Shifts in demand, the rate at which supply may be extended, the prices of available substitutes, the price – volume relationship, and the availability of future alternatives should all be considered when pricing the services. Customers' perceptions of service costs are critical for service providers to understand.

Objectives of Pricing of Services

Before determining the price of the product, targets of pricing should be clearly stated.Five main objectives of pricing are:

1. **Obtaining a Target Return on Investments:**
   his is the most crucial goal that any company strives for. The goal is to obtain a specific rate of return on investment and to structure the pricing policy to achieve that rate. For example, the company may have set a target of a 20% return on investment and a 10% after-tax return on investment. Short-term (typically a year) or long-term goals might be set.

It's a good idea to set a long-term goal.

It has been noticed that real profit rates are sometimes higher than the desired return. This is due to the fact that the previously set targets are low, and fresh prospects and demand for the product exceed the previously set return rate.

2. **Price Stability:**

Another major goal of a business is to maintain price stability. The effectiveness of a company is shown in its pricing stability over time. In practise, however, price consistency is impossible to accomplish due to fluctuating costs. Every vendor seeks to keep prices stable in a market where there are few sellers. One producer sets the price, and the rest follow suit. In terms of price fixing, he is a leader.

3. **Obtaining Market Share:**

Market share refers to the company's share of total product sales in the market. When introducing a product into a competitive market, some companies are concerned about gaining a specific market share in the early stages. In the long run, the company may try to gain a significant share of the market by selling its goods at lower rates. The major goal of gaining a higher market share is to gain a better reputation and goodwill among the public. The removal of competitors from the market is another element of extending markets through lowering prices. It's been noted that firms may be hesitant to expand the size of their stake on account of the increased risk.Fear of the government, intervention, and control General Motors, America's largest automaker, which controls almost half of the market, went through this period. Some corporations, such as General Electric and Johns-Mauville, would rather have a little market share, say 20%, than a large market share, say 50%.

4. **Competition Deterrence:**

The modern industrial setup is facing against fierce competition. Pricing can be one of the most effective tools for combating competitiveness and company rivalries. Some businesses charge lower pricing in order to keep their competitors out of the market. However, a company cannot afford to charge lower pricing for an extended length of time.

5. **Profit Maximization:**

One of the primary goals of any firm is to maximise profits. A company can establish a pricing policy that ensures more earnings. However, such businesses are also expected to fulfil certain societal responsibilities.

Pricing of administrations

Pricing is an indispensable territory in advertising. Cost is one of the huge components in the showcasing blend. It is the sole and a significant component in the showcasing blend of a firm that carries income to the business. Associations should utilize a modern way to deal with valuing. While valuing the administrations, due respect ought to be given to shifts sought after, the rate at which supply can be extended, costs of accessible substitutes, the cost – volume relationship and the accessibility of future substitutes. Administration organizations should see how clients see costs of administrations.

Problems in Marketing Services:

1. A help can't be illustrated.
2. Deal, creation and utilization of administrations happens all the while.
3. A help can't be put away. It can't be delivered fully expecting request.
4. Administrations can't be ensured through licenses.
5. Administrations can't be isolated from the specialist co-op.
6. Administrations are not normalized and are conflicting.
7. Specialist organizations naming franchisees may deal with issues of nature of administrations.
8. The client view of administration quality is all the more straightforwardly connected to the confidence, inspiration and ability of the bleeding edge staff of any help association.

Important Questions:

1. Define service marketing
2. Define product marketing
3. Define pricing
4. What is product?
5. Write down the objectives of pricing
6. Explain the difference between product marketing and service marketing

7. Write down the objective of service marketing
8. What are the seven P's of product marketing?
9. Explain in detail : problem of service marketing
10. Short notes on Profit Maximization and Price Stability
11. Explain the function of service marketing
12. List down the importance of service marketing
13. List down the Objectives of Pricing of Services
14. What is pricing of services?

V

Sales Promotion

Introduction:

Other than advertising, publicity/public relations, and personal selling, sales promotion is one of the promotional mixes. The efforts are made to improve sales by encouraging everyone engaged in the product sales process. Salespeople, dealers, and consumers are the main players in the sales process. The sales marketing activities are aimed at them in order to get them to buy by offering various incentives or rewards.

The goal of promotional activities is to get a short-term result. When a firm wants to enhance the sales of its products or services, it employs a variety of strategies. Sales promotion is when efforts other than advertising and personal selling are made. Marketing tactics that encourage targeted parties to purchase things in exchange for a bonus or reward. Customers, salespeople, and traders of various sorts are all involved in sales promotion. They each have a particular function to perform in the sales process.

Customers are the end users, and salespeople work hard to persuade them to acquire and utilise things for themselves or their families. They will be driven by additional perks, which will raise the relative value of their money. The sales force is the second party. They must be motivated in order to put out their best efforts in order to maintain a proper relationship between the firm and its traders, as well as between the company and its consumers. So that sales may be boosted, timely information, assistance, and product supply are maintained.

Consumers, wholesalers, retailers, and other organisational clients may be offered additional value or incentives in order to increase rapid sales through sales promotion. These efforts may be made in an attempt to persuade customers to purchase items or use services. Price or quantity off, coupons, discounts, samples, premiums, point-of-purchase (POP) displays, contests, scratch cards, gifts, rebates, and other sales promotion strategies are examples.

Sales promotions provide a clear incentive to act by delivering additional value beyond what is included into the product at its regular price. These transitory incentives are frequently presented at a time and location when a purchase decision is being made. Sales promotions are not only widespread in today's competitive industry, but they are also expanding at a rapid rate. These promotions are a kind of direct bribery. Despite their simplicity, sales promotions are a complex marketing tool with countless creative possibilities limited only by the creativity of promotion strategists. 'Extra purchase value' and 'below-the-line selling' are two terms used to describe sales promotion. Companies in practically every industry now have some form of promotion programme. Automobiles to drinks, financial services to meals, household durables to services, household items to business products, personal care to textiles and clothes are among the industries represented.

Sales promotions are utilised by a wide range of companies in both the consumer and commercial markets, however consumer goods marketers use them more frequently and spend more money. According to the Promotion Marketing Association, sales promotion spending in the United States alone outnumbers advertising spending.

Definitions of Sales Promotion:

According to American Marketing Associations, Sales promotion is defined as, "those marketing activities, other than personal selling, advertising and publicity that stimulates consumer purchasing and other dealer effectiveness measures such as displays, shows, expositions, demonstrations and various other non-recurrent selling efforts not in ordinary routine"

It may also be defined as "any steps taken for the purpose of obtaining or increasing sales.

Sales promotion may also be defined as all the marketing and promotional activities other than advertising, personal selling and publicity that motivate and encourage the consumer to purchase by means of such inducements as premiums, refunds, rebates, displays and demonstrations.

Sales promotion's objectives:

Sales promotion serves as a critical link between personal selling and advertising. The following goals are pursued by sales promotion activities:

1. To boost sales through publicity in the media, this is in addition to press and poster advertising.
2. To communicate information through salespeople, dealers, and others in order to guarantee that the product is used satisfactorily by the end users.
3. Encourage customers to make purchases right at the point of sale.
4. Encourage existing consumers to make more purchases.
5. To present new items to the market.
6. To bring in new clients.
7. To effectively compete against others.
8. To see whether there is a seasonal drop in sales volume.

Need of Sales Promotion

The role of sales marketing has risen dramatically in recent years. Thousands of rupees are spent on sales marketing activities in order to attract customers in our nation and throughout the world.

Some major corporations have begun to hire sales promotion managers to handle a variety of promotional materials. All of these statistics indicate that the importance of sales marketing activities is rapidly expanding. If a company's products do not sell in the market, it will fail. As a result, all marketing operations are carried out with the goal of increasing sales:

- **From the Point of View of Manufacturers:** Manufacturers need to promote their products because: It aids in the rise of sales in a competitive market, and hence profits; It aids in the introduction of new items to the market by attracting potential clients' attention; Existing stockpiles can be easily disposed of when a new product is released or when customer tastes or trend change. It maintains sales volume by keeping clients on board.
- **From the Point of View of Consumers:** Consumers benefit from sales promotions because: The consumer saves money by purchasing the product; It provides financial assistance to clients by awarding prizes and transporting them to various locations; the consumer receives complete information about the quality, characteristics, and applications of various items; Certain schemes, like as a money-back guarantee, instill

trust in customers' minds about the quality of goods; It contributes to the improvement of people's living standards. They can utilise the most recent products offered in the market by swapping their old ones.

- **From the Point of View of middlemen:** For intermediaries, sales marketing is critical because: It aids in the sale of the goods; in fact, it complements the job of a salesperson. It aids intermediaries in raising their sales. It becomes more convenient for intermediaries to sell the goods to the customers when the manufacturers use sales promotion techniques. It improves the middlemen's reputation. It aids in the increase of a middleman's profits. It provides a variety of monetary and non-monetary incentives to intermediaries.

Methods of Sales Promotions:

A range of tools and tactics are accessible to a marketer who uses sales promotion. Letters of sales promotion, catalogues, point-of-purchase displays, customer service programmes, demonstrations, free samples, discounts, contests, sweepstakes, rewards, and coupons are all frequent sales promotion techniques.

1. **Customer Promotion Methods:** The marketing of consumers Methods of sales promotion are those that actively persuade customers to buy more and more of a product.

The following are some examples of these methods:

i. **Free Sample Distribution:** The producer uses this strategy to give out free product samples to customers. They're also assigned the task of launching a new product and expanding the market. When a product is new to clients, it raises sales volume. When a product is purchased frequently, such as soaps, detergents, tea, and coffee, it is an effective device. It's a way of generating demand. Consumers can use sampling to compare items to other alternatives. Medical reps hand out samples to doctors. Teachers are provided sample copies of the books. The objective is that they will promote these goods to patients or pupils to utilise.

ii. **Coupons:** Products are accompanied by coupons. A coupon is a voucher that lowers the price of anything. When a customer presents a coupon to a retailer, he receives a discount on the merchandise (Regular price is Rs.100; with a coupon it may be Rs.80). Retailers accept coupons (which are the same as money) as payment. For the most part, coupons serve two purposes for the manufacturer. To begin with, they encourage customers to take advantage of the deal. Second, they act as a persuasion for the channel to stock the things.

iii. **PriceReduction or Promotional Discount:** It boosts sales during a slow period. It provides consumers with a temporary discount, i.e. items are sold at a lower price than the labeled price. During the wet and cold seasons, fans are sold at a lower price.

iv. **Contests:** Producers hold several contests in order to promote sales. Customers are asked questions in these tournaments. Customers are sometimes given photographs to test their general knowledge, and they are requested to offer a comprehensive description of the pictures. Customers are not paid a price to participate in these tournaments. They must, however, deliver the product's empty packets, a cash memo, the stipulated entry information form, and any other essential information. The goal of these tournaments is to identify new clients and spread the word about a new product.

v. **Exercising a Demonstration:** It is the instruction that instructs customers on how to use the product properly. It's a marketing strategy for attracting customers' attention. Demonstrations are required for sophisticated and technological items, such as computers, field gear, electrical pumping sets, and so on. In retail businesses, demonstrations of mixers and wet grinders are performed in front of customers.

vi. **High-end:** The premium strategy is also employed to entice customers to purchase the goods. In this strategy, customers are given a complimentary product in addition to the one they have purchased. This is an efficient strategy for sales marketing that is still used today.

vii. **Money-Back Guarantees:** It is the most significant sales advertising approach. Money is reimbursed if the purchaser is dissatisfied with the goods. It's written on the box. It attracts new customers and reinforces brand loyalty.

viii. **Expositions and Fairs:** India has a variety of fairs and exhibitions at various periods throughout the year. Fairs and exhibits are held on a local, regional, state, national, and even worldwide scale. Businesspeople and manufacturers present their wares at these fairs and exhibits. Due to the vast number of people who attend these fairs and exhibits, businesspeople and manufacturers have a wonderful opportunity to advertise their products.

1. **Dealer Promotion Techniques:** Dealer marketing strategies are another name for trade promotion methods. All tactics used to encourage dealers and distributors to buy and resell the product in larger and larger quantities are included in this category.The following are some of the strategies used by dealers to promote themselves:

i. **Competitions:** This strategy is intended to energies and motivates distributors, dealers, salespeople, and others. This is a non-direct method of increasing sales. This form of competition is held between merchants and wholesalers. This might take the shape of a window display, a retail display, or sales (volume), among other things. Outstanding achievements are recognised with a reward.

ii. **Discount for Purchasing Allowance:** The manufacturer's sales and the dealer's earnings both benefit from the buying allowance discount. The purchasing allowance or discount may be based on a defined percentage of the minimum amount of the product purchased over a certain time period.

iii. **High-end:** A premium is a valuable item or other incentive provided in exchange for the purchase of a product or service.Wholesalers utilise premiums to entice merchants to promote or push their items. Premiums are used to achieve a variety of goals.

   a. Persuade customers to move from a competitor's product to that of the vendor;

   b. Encourage customers to try greater product sizes.

   c. Increase sales during the off-season,

   d. Launch a new product.

iv. **Financial incentive:** Producers advertise various incentives to the dealer in this approach. It's also a powerful instrument for boosting sales. For this reason, if dealers meet their pre-determined goals, they are awarded extra awards.

v. **Access to Credit:** This system allows the producer to give credit to their dealers based on the quantity they purchased. They will be able to buy in bulk as a result of this.

vi. **Allowance for Advertising:** The dealer is also provided an advertising allowance under trade promotion strategies. The dealer is given a stipend to show the manufacturer's product at the store.

vii. **Present:** Producers employ this strategy to provide merchants with appealing and useful items in exchange for their orders. The items include transistors, radios, television sets, clocks, and watches, among others. Some manufacturers reward dealers who place more orders with complimentary vacation family excursions.

viii. **Education:** Producers use this strategy to teach their dealers so that they can quickly and seamlessly sell more and more items.

3. **Combined Promotion Methods:** For sales promotion, consumer and trade promotion methods are used together. Both of these strategies are useful in conjunction with one another. The first is a consumer promotion strategy that encourages customers to buy. The second strategy is trade promotion, which helps to grow the firm.

Both techniques of promotion are required for the success of any firm. Consumer marketing is essential for trade promotion to succeed. Similarly, consumer promotions cannot function without trade promotion. They are not antagonistic to one another, but rather complementary. Because a man requires two legs to walk, both are required for advancement. If there is a balance in the planning of these two promotions, sales promotion work may be done. As a result, consumer promotion and trade promotion are both important.

4. **Sales Force Promotion Methods:** In order to improve sales, sales force promotion schemes are required. The following are some of the instruments that may be used to promote a sales force:

i. **Bonus:** This is a monetary incentive provided to salespeople who exceed their quota or goal sales. The manufacturer establishes a sales target for the coming year. Bonuses are paid to salespeople who sell items over the desired figures.

ii. **Competitions:** Competitions encourage salespeople to sell more things. This technique is used to boost sales. Prizes are awarded to salespeople who achieve the highest sales in sales competitions for this reason.

Advertisements

The term advertising derives from the Latin word "advertere," which means "to direct people's attention." Among the definitions offered by various authors are the following:

"Advertising comprises of all the acts involved in conveying to an audience a non-personal, sponsor-identified, paid-for message about a product or organisation," writes William J. Stanton.

"Advertising is any paid type of non-personal presentation and promotion of ideas, commodities, and services by an acknowledged sponsor," according to the American Marketing Association.

Advertising is a method of disseminating information about a company to current and potential clients. It generally contains information about the advertising business, its product attributes, and the location where its items are available, among other things. Both merchants and buyers need to advertise their products. It is, nevertheless, more crucial for the sellers. Producers in the present era of large-scale production cannot imagine promoting their products without advertising them. Personal selling is supplemented to a large extent by advertising. In today's world, where there is fierce market rivalry and rapid technological advances, we discover fashion and taste in customers, advertising has become quite important.

Definitions of Advertising:

1. American Marketing Association has defined advertising as "any paid form of non-personal presentation of ideas, goods and services by an identified sponsor".

2. According to Webstar, "Advertising is to give public notice or to announce publicity".

3. According to Gardner, "Advertising is the means of mass selling that has grown up parallel with and has been made necessary to mass production".

Objectives of advertising:

Advertising's primary goal is to sell anything, whether it's a commodity, a service, or a concept. Advertising is utilised by modern corporate businesses for a variety of specialised aims in addition to this broad goal, as noted below:

1. To debut a new product by raising enthusiasm for it among the possible clients.
2. To assist personal selling programme. Advertising might be used to get customers to open their doors to salespeople.
3. To reach out to folks who are inaccessible to salespeople.
4. To break into a new market or establish a new consumer base.

5. To enhance sales by reducing market rivalry, as demonstrated in the severe struggle between Coke and Pepsi.
6. To improve the company's reputation by guaranteeing higher-quality items.

Kinds of Advertisement:

1. Display Ads - This covers internet and newspaper advertising. Digital advertisements are the latest version of newspaper advertising; it's the same principle but in 21st-century form. It entails purchasing ad space on websites that cater to your target market. Text advertising, which resembles conventional print media ads, a floating banner above the site's contact information, and even wallpaper with your product or service on the site backdrop, are all options. The utilisation of search engine optimization tactics to reach your target audiences more successfully when they search for you is the main distinction between display advertisements and newspaper ads. These sorts of ads are often also Pay per Click, which means you bid on terms most connected with your service

2. Social Media Ads - Pinterest, Instagram, Facebook, and almost all other social media platforms provide reasonably priced advertising. Paid social media advertising are the type of ad that focuses on reaching your target audience, with the amount you pay based on how many people see it and interact with it. The type of advertisement that creates a lot of word-of-mouth is organic social media ads. Let's say you post something to your company's Facebook page offering a free product in exchange for followers like and tagging a friend - that's the kind of free marketing that gets people interested in what you have to offer.

3. Newspapers and Magazines - These types of commercials are old fashioned, yet they are still effective. A excellent marketing campaign plan is to combine this form of advertisement with local, statewide, and national print media. Many individuals still read the newspaper in the morning or like curling up with a printed copy of a magazine. Furthermore, most print media now has a web presence and may integrate these sorts of ads with its digital form.

4. Outdoor Advertising - Billboards have become a big means to make an impact now that they are digital. Advertise your product or service on buses, taxis, bike messenger services, and pedicels, all of which fall under the umbrella of outdoor advertising. This method of promotion provides you fantastic brand awareness because these types of adverts are visible all over the place on a regular basis, making your product difficult to forget.

5. Radio and Podcasts - Verbal promotion is a sort of advertising that can be heard on the radio or as part of a podcast. You may have a typical style of advertisement recorded to be aired, or you can get sponsorship. For generating the sort of advertisement clients enjoy and remember, narrow down the types of podcasts your target audience subscribes to or the station they most listen to.

6. Direct Mail and Personal Sales - Small companies might benefit from direct mail, which is the art of delivering a convincing sales letter to your target audience via snail mail. To begin, determine your target market and then make an intriguing offer to all of those individuals. Measuring the replies allows you to identify which kind of clients are reacting to this format, allowing you to target your next mailing with even more accuracy. Direct or personal sales, in a similar spirit, are still a large part of promotion, especially for small enterprises. A competent salesperson can persuade a consumer to buy a product by using his or her talents. The consumer will continue to spread the word if the salesman is very effective.

7. Video Ads - On a digital level, this form of marketing engages your target clients. Create a short video and share it on social media, or pay for it to be broadcast on YouTube, Hulu, and blogs. A video ad may be developed by professionals from an agency or by your own in-house team – even if that team is just you.

8. Product Placement - This type of commercial is becoming increasingly common. Product placement occurs when you pay a podcast presenter to advertise your product or a television show to showcase a character talking about or utilising your service. You may also discuss this form of advertisement with renowned YouTube channel hosts.

9. Event Marketing - Event marketing includes paying to support a sports team or a charitable function. Because of these forms of ads, a significant number of people will hear your brand name and identify it with that particular event. For this type of niche advertising, many companies turn to conventions.

10. Email Marketing - Email marketing is a type of advertising that includes existing clients signing up for special deals or newsletters centered on your brand. When you treat consumers as insiders with VIP information, email marketing is an upgraded customer loyalty campaign that performs really effectively.

There are as many different methods to use different sorts of advertising as there are different types of advertising. You can grow by leaps and bounds by diversifying your approaches in the traditional and digital worlds, focusing on your core target market while spreading the word about your brand to the general public, and focusing on your core target market while spreading the word about your brand to the general public.

Product Advertising:

The goal of product advertising is to generate demand for a product. This involves raising customer awareness of a certain product and cultivating their interest in it. Product advertising also aims to inspire consumers to make rapid purchasing decisions based on what they see.

Forms of Product Advertising Comparative, competitive, and pioneering product advertising are the three forms of product advertising. Businesses must choose an advertising approach depending on their overall promotional goals.

Example of Product Advertising is Product advertising is a form of paid promotion that aims to persuade people to buy a product. Television, radio, print media, websites, social media, and billboards are all examples of communication channels used for product promotion.

Non- Product Advertisement:

Advertisements are designed to sell something to a certain audience, but they don't necessarily include a product for sale. Non-product advertising is a sort of marketing in which a company tries to promote an idea that it believes is significant. This style of advertisement frequently focuses on features of a firm that go beyond conventional commercial activities. Various organisations utilise non-product advertising to raise public awareness of issues or activities.

When a brand seeks to promote an idea, concept, or interest that it believes is essential and will resonate with the target audience, this is known as non-product advertising. To put it another way, it's marketing without displaying the goods.

The difference between product advertising and Non – product advertising: Advertisements are designed to sell something to a target audience, but they don't necessarily include a product to sell. This style of advertisement frequently focuses on features of a firm that go beyond conventional commercial activities. Various organisations utilise non-product advertising to raise public awareness of issues or activities.

Manufacture's own Advertisement:

Industrial advertising is typically put in industry-specific channels, allowing corporations to target specific enterprises that use their goods and services. Trade displays and business fairs are examples of these outlets. Trade journals and websites are examples of industry publications. Industrial advertising is used to advertise products and services to businesses that will use them. Industrial advertising can refer to advertising targeted towards manufacturers purchasing raw materials or equipment for their industrial processes, or it can apply to any business-to-business (B2B) advertising.

A corporation with an office, for example, will need to acquire computers, industry-specific software, and engage a cleaning service. Mowers, shovels, trimmers, a cargo trailer, and other gear are needed by a lawn-care firm. Every project necessitates the use of raw materials such as pipes and timber by a building business.

Businesses, like consumers, want their purchases to answer a specific need. They like to see advertisements about answers to their issues rather than advertisements about the company selling the product.

Unlike individual customers who frequently browse around for one-time offers or irregular purchases, corporations frequently require the same items. They seek a long-term partnership with a vendor so that obtaining the products they require becomes a predictable component of their business strategy.

The goal of industrial advertising is to interact with companies and persuade them to buy something. Industrial advertisements are used to attract customers, enhance sales, extend distribution channels, and raise brand recognition.

Types of Manufacture' own Advertising:

Industrial advertising, like other forms of advertising, should be based on a marketing strategy that includes data on your target customers, competitors, market, and unique selling proposition. These aspects enable you to pinpoint the most effective ways to reach out to firms that require your services.

Industrial advertising is typically put in industry-specific channels, allowing corporations to target specific enterprises that use their goods and services. These are some of the channels available:

- Business fairs or trade exhibitions
- Trade journals and websites are examples of industry publications.

- Brochures, postcards, and catalogues are examples of direct mail ads.
- Making a cold call or sending an email
- Referral marketing or word-of-mouth

Remember that professionals who make logistical choices for their firms will not receive their information from the same places that consumers do when creating a marketing campaign that incorporates industrial advertising. Manufacturing equipment and office supplies are not marketed on television since the majority of viewers will not require them. Instead, industrial advertising should be properly placed to represent your company as the industry's leading solution.

Customers in the industrial sector often want to learn more about the products they're evaluating. One approach to simultaneously educate and advertise is through content marketing. Content marketing entails providing businesses with appealing content. If you're a tech business that provides software to manufacturers, for example, you might produce a blog article on the indicators that their programme needs to be updated.

Advertisement Agencies

An advertising agency is a self-contained business that provides specialised services in advertising and marketing in general. The term "agency" is now a legal oxymoron.

These businesses are not agents in the legal sense, but rather self-contained businesses. Advertising agencies began as space brokers, arranging for the placement of advertisements in newspapers. The agencies' functions, on the other hand, have evolved with time. They are now primarily responsible for serving advertisements rather than assisting the media.

It represents the advertiser, who is a manufacturer, wholesaler, or retailer, as an agent or consultant. In the legal sense, it is not an agent. Initially, it served as a space broker for advertising placed in the media owner's publications, such as newspapers.

The Function of Advertising Agencies

- Creating a commercial based on the facts acquired about the product, conducting research about the company, the product, and consumer reactions.
- Planning for the sort of media to be utilised, when and where it will be used, and for how long it will be used are all important considerations.

- Taking input from both clients and consumers and then deciding on the next course of action
- This is something that any company can undertake on their own. They can create advertising, print them, and broadcast them on television or other media; they can also maintain the accounts. The following are the reasons why businesses hire advertising agencies.

There are five different sorts of advertising agency.

1. **Service in its entirety Agencies**

   - Large-scale firms.
   - Deals with the entire advertising process.
   - For each department, there are various experts.
   - Work begins with data collection and analysis and concludes with payment of invoices to media personnel.

2. **Interactive Advertising Agencies**

   - Modern communication methods are applied.
   - Uses internet marketing, mobile phone personal communications, and other methods.
   - The commercials created are very interactive, include novel themes, and are highly inventive.

3. **Boutiques that are innovative**

   - Ads those are both imaginative and unique.
   - Apart from producing adverts, no other function is performed.
   - Smaller agency with in-house copywriters, directors, and creative.

4. **Media Buying Firms**

   - Purchases advertising space and sells it to marketers.
   - Sells the amount of time that advertising will be displayed.
   - Schedules time slots on various television and radio stations.
   - Finally, supervises or verifies whether the advertisement was broadcast at the desired time and location.

5. **In-House Advertising Agencies**

- It's on par with full-service agencies.
- These kinds of agencies, which are in-house and work only for them, are preferred by large corporations.
- These businesses operate in accordance with the needs of their clients.

Telemarketing:

Direct marketing includes telemarketing. Telemarketing is the marketing contact between buyers and sellers using current telecommunications technologies such as the telephone, fax (tax), television, computer, and Internet. The maker advertises the product, its characteristics, usage, pricing, and availability on television through telemarketing. Customers who are interested in placing orders with the manufacturer can do so by mail, telephone, or other means. The deliveries are made via a carrier, mail, or other means.

For consumers in the United States, Harrod's of London has an international 800 number, and IBM utilises it in Europe. Some groups have condemned telemarketing for invading people's privacy and using high-pressure techniques. Telemarketing, on the other hand, has gained in popularity as a result of the convenience it gives as well as the cost and time savings it delivers to the consumer.

International marketing has been transformed by telemarketing. It is now simple to locate and profile consumers or suppliers all around the world. This has added a new dimension to global rivalry.

When a small business's products or services have hard-to-reach clients, or when many prospects must be reached in order to identify one interested in making a purchase, telemarketing comes in handy.

Product marketing is an example of telemarketing. A caller in product marketing is responsible for bringing a product to market, releasing a new product, technology, or brand, and alerting people about it to stimulate customer interest.

Benefits of Telemarketing:

- Telemarketing's advantages include a more involved and personalised sales experience.
- Immediately establish a connection with your consumers.

- Explain technical concerns in a more straightforward manner.
- create appointments and leads
- To expand your sales zone, sell from afar.
- More clients can be reached than with in-person sales calls.

Advantages and disadvantages of Telemarketing:

Telemarketing refers to the practice of selling goods and services via the phone. It has both advantages and disadvantages. The advantages are that it is simple to reach out to clients and, if done correctly, it is cost effective and disadvantages it has a poor reputation, and some of the initial expenditures are too expensive.

E- Marketing:

E-Marketing (Electronic Marketing), often known as Internet Marketing, Web Marketing, Digital Marketing, or Online Marketing, is internet-based marketing. E-marketing is the practise of using the Internet to sell a product or service offering to a target audience via cellphones, gadgets, social media, and other means. E-marketing encompasses not just online marketing but also e-mail and cellular marketing. It makes use of a variety of technologies to help businesses interact with their consumers.

E-marketing, like many other media channels, is an element of integrated marketing communications (IMC), which aids a brand's growth across many channels. Companies that use a variety of digital media platforms have turned to e-marketing as a key component of their marketing strategy.

Importance of E-marketing

In today's world, when the majority of work and transactions are conducted online, it is critical for marketers to reach out to customers through the appropriate channels. Smartphones, tablets, smart TVs, laptops are being used internationally to operate companies and purchase and sell commodities. E-marketing enables you to reach out to your audience through various platforms as well as traditional offline methods. E-marketing is often the only realistic choice for certain products. When compared to offline marketing, the efficacy of e-marketing is quite clear. One feature that distinguishes e-marketing is the ability to track the impact in real time. When opposed to offline marketing, marketers can observe how well their campaigns are performing and adjust their messaging accordingly. When offline or traditional marketing channels are unable to provide the best return on investment during a pandemic, internet marketing becomes even more important.

Advantages of E-marketing

The following are some of the advantages of e-marketing:

- It has a much higher return on investment than traditional marketing because it helps increase sales revenue.
- E-marketing refers to the use of the internet to conduct marketing campaigns at a lower cost.
- The campaign's results are quick since it helps to target the proper clients.
- Web tracking features make e-marketing more productive by allowing for easy monitoring.
- Viral content may be created through e-marketing, which aids viral marketing.

Types of e-marketing

Companies may utilise the internet for marketing in a variety of ways. E-marketing may be done in a variety of ways, including:

- Article promotion
- Affiliate marketing is number two.
- Video marketing
- Newsletters and email marketing
- Blogging
- Content marketing
- Podcasts
- Webinars

All of these and other strategies aid in e-marketing and contacting customers over the internet for a company or brand.

E-Marketing Examples

A 360-degree campaign done by a company that uses both direct and indirect marketing channels to spread the message is an excellent example. Newsletters, videos, podcasts, and webinars are all examples of e-Marketing that are targeted directly to potential consumers. Customers also learn about the brand and goods through indirect marketing channels such as social media connections, content marketing, and thought leadership. All of these channels are entirely accessible over the internet.

These campaigns might include offline counterparts that carry the same message, or they could be entirely driven by e-marketing. Many businesses are increasingly heavily relying on internet platforms to sell their goods. Apple, Samsung, and other major phone makers broadcast their new product debuts live across the world, revealing new features and price for forthcoming phones and other products. Even in the gaming industry, there are several online events where forthcoming titles are showcased to the public.

Important Questions:

1. Define advertising
2. Define advertising objective.
3. Define sales promotion
4. What is product?
5. What is non product?
6. What is advertising?
7. List down the need of sales promotion
8. Explain the methods of sales promotion
9. Write down the kinds of advertisements
10. Give examples of product advertisement
11. Explain manufacture own advertisements
12. Write down the types of manufacturing own advertisements
13. What is advertisement agencies explain in detail?
14. Explain the function of advertising agencies.
15. Explain telemarketing and its benefits.
16. Explain the advantages and disadvantages of telemarketing
17. What is E- Marketing?
18. Explain the importance of E-Marketing
19. Write down the types of E- Marketing?
20. What all are the advantages of E- Marketing